Palgrave Studies in Sound

Series Editor
Mark Grimshaw-Aagaard
Musik
Aalborg University
Aalborg, Denmark

Palgrave Studies in Sound is an interdisciplinary series devoted to the topic of sound with each volume framing and focusing on sound as it is conceptualized in a specific context or field. In its broad reach, Studies in Sound aims to illuminate not only the diversity and complexity of our understanding and experience of sound but also the myriad ways in which sound is conceptualized and utilized in diverse domains. The series is edited by Mark Grimshaw-Aagaard, The Obel Professor of Music at Aalborg University, and is curated by members of the university's Music and Sound Knowledge Group.

Editorial Board:

Mark Grimshaw-Aagaard (series editor)
Martin Knakkergaard
Mads Walther-Hansen

Editorial Committee:

Michael Bull
Barry Truax
Trevor Cox
Karen Collins

Vadim Keylin

Participatory Sound Art

Technologies, Aesthetics, Politics

Vadim Keylin
Institute for German Language and Literature
University of Hamburg
Hamburg, Germany

ISSN 2633-5875 ISSN 2633-5883 (electronic)
Palgrave Studies in Sound
ISBN 978-981-99-6356-0 ISBN 978-981-99-6357-7 (eBook)
https://doi.org/10.1007/978-981-99-6357-7

© The Editor(s) (if applicable) and The Author(s), under exclusive licence to Springer Nature Singapore Pte Ltd. 2023
This work is subject to copyright. All rights are solely and exclusively licensed by the Publisher, whether the whole or part of the material is concerned, specifically the rights of translation, reprinting, reuse of illustrations, recitation, broadcasting, reproduction on microfilms or in any other physical way, and transmission or information storage and retrieval, electronic adaptation, computer software, or by similar or dissimilar methodology now known or hereafter developed.
The use of general descriptive names, registered names, trademarks, service marks, etc. in this publication does not imply, even in the absence of a specific statement, that such names are exempt from the relevant protective laws and regulations and therefore free for general use.
The publisher, the authors, and the editors are safe to assume that the advice and information in this book are believed to be true and accurate at the date of publication. Neither the publisher nor the authors or the editors give a warranty, expressed or implied, with respect to the material contained herein or for any errors or omissions that may have been made. The publisher remains neutral with regard to jurisdictional claims in published maps and institutional affiliations.

This Palgrave Macmillan imprint is published by the registered company Springer Nature Singapore Pte Ltd.
The registered company address is: 152 Beach Road, #21-01/04 Gateway East, Singapore 189721, Singapore

Paper in this product is recyclable.

Acknowledgements

This book is the result of a six-year undertaking that has seen me move cities and countries during a pandemic. It would not have been possible without the support from many wonderful people, and I would like to express my most heartfelt thanks to:

My PhD supervisor Iben Have, whose gentle guidance, constructive criticism and unflinching encouragement have helped my growth immensely and showed me what true mentorship is.

My Shut Up & Write group, without whom I would have spent all these years staring at a blank page.

Benoît Maubrey, Katrine Faber, Kaffe Matthews and other amazing artists, whose work inspired this book.

My dear friend Olga, who had me started on the academic path and has been a beacon of emotional support through good and bad times alike.

All of my wonderful friends and loved ones.

About the Book

The issues of interactivity and participation have been widely present in sound art since its very inception. They are often mentioned in artists' interviews and statements and form the cornerstones of many sound art practices. Yet despite the obvious importance participation has for sound artists and despite the growing prominence of both sound art and participatory art during the past decades, the position of participatory sound art in scholarship remains marginal. Sound art studies typically prioritise the material aspects of sonic medium—its sensory qualities as a modality of perception, its corporeal effects as a mechanical vibration or the technological grounds of auditory culture. Conversely, the literature on participatory art has historically cast the media-specific aspects aside and focused its analyses on the social forms and processes that participatory artworks operate through and the art's role in broader socio-political context.

The book addresses this gap in literature by offering a survey of participatory practices that are specific to sound art from its origins in the historical avantgardes to grassroots, non-institutionalised forms of sonic creativity in digital participatory culture. It approaches participatory sound art from an innovative pragmatist theoretical perspective that allows to draw connections between the materiality of sound artworks and environments and the sociality of participatory activities that they facilitate. This framework takes at its core John Dewey's understanding of art experience as always proceeding in cycles of doing and undergoing and builds upon three principal concepts: affordance, perspective and gesture, each explored in relation to sound art in a dedicated chapter. The notion of affordance is adopted from James Gibson's project of ecological psychology; it allows to examine the ways the artwork's materialities facilitate, guide or restrict participation. G.H. Mead's idea of perspective as the structuring principle of perceptual reality informed by the way one intends to act is used to trace the network of creative agencies, both human and material, involved in a participatory sound art situation. Finally, the book applies performance scholar Sruti Bala's theory of gesture as an action suspended between the physical, the symbolic and the social to explore the political aspects of participation in sound art.

In considering these connections the book contributes to the growing fields of both sound studies and participation studies, as well as to curatorial practice regarding sound art and participatory art. It introduces a number of previously underrepresented practices into sound art history, while reassessing the role of others, rethinking the development of the art form from the perspective of its sociality and its relation to sociality of music. At the same time, the book questions the dominant narratives of participatory art by considering how the particular materialities and medialities of sound reshape the processes of participation. Moreover, the applications of the theory of sonic pragmatism developed in the book are not limited to sound art proper and have implications for a broader range of phenomena and practices of sonic culture, such as sound design, sonic branding, sound synthesis and others.

Finally, the research represented in the book has practical applications. It provides insights into the operations of participatory sound artworks and the audience's engagement with them that could be useful to institutions exhibiting and curating sound art and/or participatory art. But furthermore, the book's analyses of the participants' experience with sound artworks, their potential uses and political aspects could be applied in a broader context, e.g., to acoustic design of public spaces and public institutions.

Contents

1 **Introduction** 1
 1.1 Sound Art and Participation 1
 1.2 Sound, Art, Music 8
 1.3 Participation, Interactivity, Collaboration 14
 References 16

2 **Histories** 21
 2.1 Sound, Participation and Gesamtkunstwerk 21
 2.2 Sound and Participation in Historical Avantgarde 23
 2.3 Sound and Participation in the Post-War Avantgarde 24
 2.4 Sound and Participation After the Cold War 30
 2.5 Interactive Audio and Digital Culture 35
 References 39

3 **Discourses** 43
 3.1 Sonic, Spatial, Social 44
 3.2 Sense Versus Senses 47
 3.3 Sonic Pragmatism 49
 3.4 Sonic Doing: Acts and Gestures 53
 3.5 Creative Undergoing: Agencies and Ecologies 57
 References 61

4	**Affordances**	65
	4.1 *Sound Artworks as Platforms*	66
	4.2 *Aesthetic Affordances*	67
	4.3 *Technological Environments*	72
	4.4 *Beyond the Artwork*	81
	4.5 *Materiality and Sociality*	84
	References	86
5	**Perspectives**	89
	5.1 *Creative Agency*	90
	5.2 Katrine Faber: *Let Us Sing Your Place*	91
	5.3 Benoît Maubrey: *Speaker Sculptures*	99
	5.4 *Perspectives on Participation*	106
	References	111
6	**Gestures**	115
	6.1 *Sonic Gestures Between Symbols and Actions*	116
	6.2 *Gestures of Concern*	119
	6.3 *Gestures of Empowerment*	123
	6.4 *Gestures of Togetherness*	128
	6.5 *Sounds of the Possible*	131
	References	133
7	**Conclusion**	137
	References	146

Index   151

About the Author

Vadim Keylin is a cultural theorist working in the fields of sound studies and digital culture. He holds a PhD in Aesthetics and Culture from Aarhus University, Denmark, and is currently employed as a research associate in the project "Poetry in the Digital Age" at the University of Hamburg. He serves as an editor of the *SoundEffects* journal and has written articles in international peer-reviewed journals such as *Organised Sound*, *Sound Studies*, *SoundEffects* and others. In addition to his research activities, Keylin has written two poetry books and participated in a number of media art and poetry festivals.

CHAPTER 1

Introduction

Abstract This chapter introduces the main themes of the book and offers an overview of the chapters. It points to a gap in academic literature: while sound art and participatory art largely developed in parallel and participation is clearly important to many sound artists (as evidenced both by their statements and their practices), the issue has been largely missing from the sound art scholarship. Furthermore, as both sound art and participation are somewhat contentious terms and subject of much debate, it overs an overview of positions on and definitions of both phenomena, developing a working definition of participatory sound art.

Keywords Sound art • Participatory art • Klangkunst • Participation • Interactivity • Pragmatism

1.1 Sound Art and Participation

Late twentieth century saw an explosion of artistic practices that took sound outside of musical venues and concert formats. Already in mid-1950s, French sculptor brothers Bernard and François Baschet began exhibiting their experimental musical instruments—sounding functionalist sculptures of metal, glass and plastic—in museums and galleries, where the public could play them. In late 1960s, American percussionist Max Neuhaus moved his activities beyond the concert stage, organising listening tours of

New York's industrial areas, call-in radio shows where he mixed in real-time the sounds that callers were submitting over phone lines, and creating the first sound installations, which he defined as sounds arranged in space instead of time, "letting the listener place them in his own time" (Neuhaus and Jardins 1994, 34). In early 1970s, artists like Peter Vogel in Europe and Liz Phillips in USA introduced cybernetic sculptures and installations that made sounds in reaction to the spectator's movements, while in Canada Hildegard Westerkamp became a champion for soundwalking. By the 1990s, these practices and many others like them—sound installations, sound sculptures, sounding performance art—have coalesced into an art form of their own, which was dubbed sound art. Over the following years, this "aggressively expanding art form" (Krogh Groth and Schulze 2020, 1) became institutionalised in a network of galleries and festivals and conceptualised through a growing corpus of academic literature, even if the exact definition of the term sound art remains contested.

While this shift from the established cultural forms and practices of music to a broader and more open-ended category of sound is by now relatively well documented (see, e.g., Motte-Haber 1999; Licht 2007, 2019; LaBelle 2015; Kelly 2017), what is largely missing from the existing accounts of sound art is the accompanying shift from reception to participation. As I will show in Chap. 2, the issues of interactivity and participation have played a prominent role in sound art ever since its very beginnings, both evident in the artworks themselves and often professed in the artists' statements and interviews. For example, the Baschet brothers, who coined the term "sound sculpture" for their works, defined them as combinations of "shapes, sounds and public participation" (Baschet and Baschet 1987, 110). Max Neuhaus (1994, n.p.) has always emphasised the element of discovery in his sound installations and positioned himself as a "catalyser of sonic activity" rather than composer or performer. Peter Vogel (1996) described his cybernetic sound objects as having a behaviour and being able to enter a dialog with the audience. Many similar statements could be cited.

Yet despite the obvious importance the phenomenon of participation has for sound artists, its position in both the academic literature on sound art and curatorial practice remains marginal. My initial impulse for this book came from my previous work on sound sculpture (Keylin 2015). Analysing the works of the Baschet brothers, Peter Vogel, Harry Bertoia and others, I was surprised by the jarring discrepancy between the prominence of participation in their practices and its absence from handbooks and other major scholarly works on sound art. It pointed to a bigger gap too—the listening-centeredness of sound art scholarship and its eliding the issues creative soundmaking.

Similarly, sound art examples are largely absent from the literature on participatory art. In the few instances sound artworks are discussed (typically in texts dealing with interactivity in new media art—e.g., Dinkla 1996; Wilson 2002; Heinrich 2014), their sonic character is not afforded any special consideration. Ostensibly (as I will elaborate in Chap. 3), this blind spot occurs due to participatory art and sound art theories having diverging perspectives on their respective practices. Sound art studies typically prioritise the material aspects of sonic medium—its sensory qualities as a modality of perception, its corporeal effects as a mechanical vibration, or the technological grounds of auditory culture (see, e.g., Motte-Haber 1999; Licht 2007; Voegelin 2010; LaBelle 2015). Conversely, the literature on participatory art has historically cast the media-specific aspects aside and focused its analyses on the level of the social—social forms and processes that participatory artworks operate through and their role in broader socio-political context (Kester 2004, 2011; Jackson 2011; Bishop 2012).

My contention is that participatory sound art demands a particular theoretical position that is fundamentally different from the approaches already existing in the literature on sound art or participatory art. First, it should consider both the sociality of sonic interactions and the material specificity of the sound medium in which they are realised. Second, catering to an aesthetic experience that primarily operates through acts of soundmaking, it should emphasise the doing—the creativity, expressivity and teleology of sound acts performed by the participants. Finally, participation being a collective endeavour, such a theory should not prioritise the subject or the object but rather focus on the relations between different actors—both human and non-human, given the importance of materiality—involved in a participatory exchange.

The goal of this book is thus twofold. First, it aims to open up the discussion on the participatory aspects of sound art, both bringing due analytical attention to a corpus of artworks often overlooked in the mainstream sound art narratives and offering new perspectives on some of the "classical" sound artworks. It bears noting, however, that the selection of artworks discussed in this book is not intended to delimit participatory sound art as a genre or to map participatory practices in sound art exhaustively. As will become clear from the following sections, such a task would be impossible. Nor is historical precedence my concern here—although Chap. 2 challenges the conventional narratives of sound art history, its goal is not to establish who did what first, but rather to point to theoretical incompleteness of these narratives. Instead, I have chosen the artworks that I find emblematic of participatory sound art, both in that they feature interactivity and participation prominently and in that they represent the diversity of forms participation may take in sound art.

Second, in discussing these artworks and issues, this book makes a case for a sound art aesthetic rooted in pragmatist philosophy. Challenging the dominant phenomenological and new materialist approaches to sound art, the aesthetic paradigm proposed here emphasises the active, expressive and teleological aspects of sound. It draws on a variety of disciplines—science and technology studies, media studies, creativity studies, music sociology and ethnomusicology—to expand the vocabulary of sound art theory and address the interpenetrations of technology, aesthetics and politics in participatory sound art.

These two goals largely determine the book's structure. In Chap. 2 I briefly trace the parallel histories of sound art and participatory art over the past hundred years, showing how participatory sensibilities have been the core aspect of sound art since its very inception. Building on Claire Bishop's (2012, Chap. 1) approach to historical categorisation, the chapter explores the relationships of sound and participation in the art practices of four periods: the historical Avantgarde, the Post-war Avantgarde, late twentieth century and the digital age. I begin by situating the common origins of sound art and participatory art in the Avantgarde interpretations of the *Gesamtkunstwerk*, with both (non-musical) sound and participation serving as means of disturbing the border between art and everyday life. In the Post-war Avantgarde, the focus of art shifts towards questioning the art object and the phenomenological explorations of the conditions of art production and reception. The ephemerality of sound and participation makes them perfect aesthetic vehicles for these explorations, leading to the creation of what is acknowledged as the first works of sound art and participatory art. In late twentieth century, the two art forms gain their discursive and institutional identities, but as a result, gravitate apart, producing the theoretical gap that this book aims to mend. Finally, the digital age brings sound and participation back together as features of digital media and digital culture—introducing a third, technological dimension to the interplay of the sensory and the social in participatory sound art.

Chapter 3 continues the discussion of the connections and frictions between sound art and participatory art, but from a theoretical rather than a historical perspective. It starts by briefly surveying the existing sound and participation literature for possible points of convergence that would allow for situating participatory sound art within these discourses. Its main aim however is the introduction of a pragmatist aesthetic of sound.

Pragmatism can be roughly described as an epistemological position that focuses on what things *do* rather than what they *are*—in other words, on actions and relations rather than subjects and objects (see Pierce 1935). As such, a pragmatist aesthetic allows attending to the interactional and expressive aspects of participatory sound art that are ill-served by the existing phenomenological and new materialist frameworks. In an earlier article, I have already proposed a pragmatist approach to sound studies in a more general sense (Keylin 2021). In Chap. 3—and this book as a whole— I offer a more specialised account of a pragmatist aesthetic of participatory sound art.

My approach builds on the classical American pragmatism of John Dewey (1930 [1916]; 1980 [1934]) and George Herbert Mead (1938, 1972 [1934]) setting it in the dialog with contemporary pragmatist approaches such as Bruno Latour's (1994, 2005) and Antoine Hennion's (2015) actor-network theory and mediation theory or James Gibson's (1979) ecological psychology, as well as with sound art and participatory art discourses. Dewey claimed that at the core of art experience is the dialectic of doing and undergoing—acting on the environment and being affected by it—which applies equally to both art production and art reception. My contention is that in participation, which combines production and reception into one process, this dialectic becomes even more pronounced. However, to account for the assemblages of human and non-human actors in participatory sound art, doing and undergoing have to be expanded into the broader category of mediation, understood as the interplay of human and non-human agencies that is characteristic of both technological interactions (Latour 1994; Born 2005) and socio-aesthetic processes such as musicking (Hennion 2015).

The second half of the chapter details three analytical categories that structure my analyses of socio-material mediations of participatory sound art in the rest of the book: affordance, perspective and gesture. Coined by Gibson (1979), the term affordance refers to the opportunities for action a situation provides an agent. The notion of perspective is used by Mead (1972 [1934]) to describe the way one's perceptual reality is structured by their intention to act in a certain way. In the context of participatory sound art, they offer two complimentary ways of approaching the interplay of material and social agencies: as action opportunities that artworks and social situations that arise from them provide (affordance), or as ways sound artworks (and situations) are (re)configured by action-orientations of the participants (perspective). Finally, I borrow the concept of gesture from Sruti Bala (2018)—who in turn draws on Marcel Mauss (1973 [1935]), Giorgio Agamben (1993, 1999) and Carrie Noland (2010)—to discuss the participants' actions and interactions themselves and the way they unfold simultaneously in the material, social and discursive planes.

The following three chapters each focus on one of these concepts. Chapter 4 considers participatory sound artworks from the perspective of affordance theory. Its central argument is that the material (sensory, technological, spatiotemporal) and social (participatory, relational) aspects of the artwork necessarily influence and inform each another. I use the concept of affordance as an analytical device to investigate how participatory processes in sound art are neither limited to the artistic intent, nor completely unconstrained, being instead delimited and directed by the artwork's materialities—which they in turn reshape. The chapter first discusses three principal affordances characteristic of participatory sound artworks in general: for creativity, experimentation and connectivity. I argue that irrespective of their specific implementations, by virtue of deviating from established models of "polite" quiet concert listening, participatory sound artworks offer the participants opportunity to express themselves creatively without the fear of being judged, which in turn facilitates openness and social exchange between them.

In the second half of the chapter, I classify sound art's materialities and medialities into three environment types—local (not technologically extended in any way), networked and augmented—exploring the affordances that stem from their specific technological organisation. While sound art in local environments relies on its immediacy and corporeality to encourage the participants to interact with the works (physically) and each other (socially), networked environments employ the network's ability to connect spaces and actors over spatial and institutional barriers to foster inclusivity and interaction across difference. At the same time, augmented sound art, introducing a virtual sonic layer to an existing physical site, expands the participants' perception and makes them engage deeper with the site and its natural, cultural and social aspects.

Finally, I consider forms of sonic participation that go beyond the artwork as a kind of fourth environment type. The affordances of mobile technologies and online media allow for sonic artworks to serve as catalysts for the participants' creativity that exceeds the borders of the art situation. Furthermore, these creative expressions informed by participatory sound art exist in a continuum with grassroots practices of sonic experimentation in participatory culture—essentially, sonic memes. While not conceptualised in terms of art and artworks, such practices exhibit the same principal affordances—for creativity, experimentation and connectivity—as participatory sound art.

While Chap. 4 discusses the material agencies of sound artworks, In Chap. 5 I turn to creative agencies and perspectives of the human actors involved in such artworks—namely, artists and participants. The central theoretical device of this discussion is G.H. Mead's (1972 [1934]) notion of perspective—the way one's perception of their immediate environment is structured by their intention to act in certain ways. The chapter further adopts creativity psychologist Vlad Glaveanu's (2018) view on perspective and taking new perspectives as a necessary condition for creative acts. As perspectives are specific to their carriers, this necessitates an empirical rather than purely analytic approach. The core of the chapter is formed by two qualitative case studies—of Katrine Faber's participatory sound performance *Let Us Sing Your Place* and Benoît Maubrey's interactive *Speaker Sculptures*—that combine interviews and ethnographic observations to investigate the interplay of creative agencies facilitated by these artworks. I further contextualise these qualitative findings within the broader spectrum of perspectives by considering, on the one hand, the statements, articles and interviews of sound artists who work with participation, and on the other hand, ethnomusicological studies of participation in traditional and experimental music.

My case studies show that participation requires neither the subjugation of the artist's own creativity, nor exerting control over the participants—rather the artists' and participants' creative agencies are exercised in different material dimensions. Largely agreeing with Alan Licht's (2019) observation that, unlike a composer, a sound artist is not a soundmaker, the artists I interviewed left the creative soundmaking to the audiences, while pursuing their aesthetic goals in the performative (Faber) or sculptural (Maubrey) aspects of their works. At the same time, for the audiences, the participatory sound art situation made them rethink a number of conventional ideas about sound and art. While not necessarily experimental music connoisseurs, they readily embraced the unusual and unmusical sounds they were making—despite these very sounds often provoking hostile responses in concert audiences. The participants' performances also lacked the narcissism and self-centredness often ascribed to contemporary culture, exhibiting altruistic and communal perspectives instead.

The final chapter considers the politics of participation in sound art. It employs Sruti Bala's (2018) theory of gesture—an action that is at the same time inherently aesthetic and socially and politically embedded—to discuss the political potentialities of sound artworks, while not limiting them to critical statements or explicitly activist projects. The chapter examines the political gestures of participatory sound art at two levels: the artworks themselves as gestures expressing a political sentiment and a political pragmatics, and the gestures of the participants performed in the context of sound artworks. I focus on three types of such gestures I consider the most important, although the list is far from being exhaustive: of concern, of empowerment and of togetherness.

I use the notion of concern—alluding to Latour's (2004) "matters of concern"—to describe a shift from intellectual critique and "didactic provocation" (Kester 2011, 9) of contemporary visual art towards facilitating affective engagement with political issues in participatory sound art. It offers the participants a unique first-person, up close and personal, perspective on the matters at hand, inviting them to address their agency and responsibility as political actors. This heightened experience of political agency may in turn foster empowerment—a category widely overused in participatory art discourse, yet still applicable as long as its limitations are considered—and a sense of community. The politics of participatory sound art can thus be described as "politics of the possible"—of enabling political imaginaries, both utopian and dystopian.

1.2 Sound, Art, Music

Before I proceed to the core of my argument, its object needs to be defined. Both "sound art" and "participation" remain rather nebulous and contested terms, making the task of explaining what I mean by "participatory sound art" in the title of this book twice as urgent—and twice as difficult.

As an ostensibly new art form that emerged in the twentieth century, sound art had to elaborate its identity against the backdrop of an established system of artistic disciplines developed in the course of centuries-long history of Western arts (Keylin 2015). As such, any definition of sound art has to consider its relation to its two Others—music (an art form that has domain over sound) and visual art (an art form that has domain over the presentational format of exhibition). On this ground, the existing definitions can be roughly classified into four categories, depending on where they situate sound art: in-between music and visual art (bridging the two), beyond music and visual art (independent from both), squarely within visual art (often rejecting sound art as a distinct art form), and squarely within music. In what follows I will discuss the various positions and their relations to the issues of participation and sociality to develop a working definition of sound art to use in the rest of the book.

The first approach, positioning sound art as a merging of visual arts and music, or even more broadly—spatial and temporal arts—is typically associated with the German scholarship. This tradition primarily has its point of departure in sound installation and sound sculpture, practices that precede sound art as a term by a couple of decades. German musicologist and pioneer of sound art studies Helga de la Motte-Haber wrote of the new art form:

> *Klangkunst* in the narrow sense is, however, mainly defined through new aesthetical implications, which have crystallised over the course of a long historical process. To this belongs an abandonment of the strong differentiation between spatial and time-based qualities, which had already been questioned by the musicalisation of painting and abolished with the onset of process art. Through this, every purist concept of the artistic material, which assumed a division between the eye and the ear, was dissolved. An art form emerged that wanted to be heard and seen at the same time. (Motte-Haber 1996, 16; English translation quoted from Engström and Stjerna 2009, 12)

The German word *Klangkunst*, left untranslated in the above quote, points to the idiosyncraticity of this approach compared to the understanding of sound art in Anglophone literature, which typically zooms in onto the innate aesthetic, perceptual or conceptual aspects of (non-musical) sound (Engström and Stjerna 2009). This discrepancy even led some scholars to consider sound art and *Klangkunst* as two distinct, if somewhat overlapping, categories (see, e.g., Czolbe 2014).

Despite the initially diverging paths of the two traditions, more recent Anglophone literature seems to have shifted towards better acknowledging and integrating the contributions of the German scholarship. *The Bloomsbury Handbook of Sound Art* (2020) edited by Sanne Krogh Groth and Holger Schulze roots its definition of the art form in de la Motte-Haber's work. Krogh Groth and Schulze (2020, 13), however, point out four problems with defining sound art squarely as something "that wanted to be heard and seen at the same time" and its positioning within a rigid system of artistic disciplines: "Euro- and Germano-centrism, ignoring the vernacular sound practices of popular culture, overly focusing on the psychology of perception, and the depoliticization of sound art". They opt instead to broaden the category of sound art almost to the point of "non-definition", emphasising that sound art "is not separated from phenomena outside the artistic work, the music culture or the art world", in contrast to Western fine art and art music traditions "where art is recognised teleologically and autonomous" (Krogh Groth and Schulze 2020, 4–5).

Overall, the Anglophone literature on sound art—being centred, as noted above, on the concept of sound—grounds its definitions largely within the sonic epistemologies rather than art theory. As such, sound art's relations to both visual art and music are de-emphasised in these approaches, situating it, as the title of Alan Licht's (2007) book suggests, "beyond music, between categories". For Christoph Cox (2009, 2018), for example, the distinction of sound art and music reflects the Deleuzian dichotomy of the virtual and the actual: where music operates through various sonic actualisations, sound art provides the listener access to the primal metaphysical flux that is sound in Cox's philosophy. At the same time, Salomé Voegelin in *Listening to Noise and Silence* (2010) bases her definitions on the dichotomy of vision—distanced, dominant and "objective"—and listening, which is necessarily embodied and embedded in the world. Paradoxically, she relegates to the realm of vision not only visual art, but also music—understood as notated Western music—as it primarily exists as texts (scores) to be read, analysed and interpreted. However, from her phenomenological position, sound art to Voegelin is a modality of perception more so than a quality of the artwork. Anything can be listened to as sound art as long as what is listened to is "the experience of sound as temporal relationship", which "is not between things but is the thing, the sound itself" (Voegelin 2010, 4–5).

Sonic epistemology and sociality of sound culture become reconciled in Brandon LaBelle's approach. For LaBelle (2015, xi), sound art is a practice that "harnesses, describes, analyses, performs, and interrogates the condition of sound", which is understood as "intrinsically and unignorably relational". However, instead of tackling this relationality of sound per se, he focuses on the spatial qualities of sound artworks, claiming that "sound as relational phenomena immediately operates through modes of spatiality". In a similar fashion, Gascia Ouzounian (2008, 2013) connects the spatiality of sound installation art to social issues by way of Henri Lefebvre's theory of space as being produced by social relationships.

While the definitions discussed so far position sound art roughly at equal (non-)distance from art and music, noticeably more effort is made to separate it from the latter—typically understood in this discussion as Western classical music. This is understandable from both historical and theoretical perspectives. On the one hand, many of sound art pioneers were composers or musicians moving into the art context to escape the institutional, presentational or market frames of music (Licht 2019). On the other hand, music arguably has a stronger claim to sound art than visual art does, which stipulates the necessity of a stronger counterargument. Finally, Western art music tradition, against which many early sound artists defined their artistic identities, imposes a certain approach to sound with its focus on abstract tones and the mathematics of composition, to the exclusion of the "extra-musical"—the contextual, the performative, the discursive—that is ostensibly the focus of sound art.

Taken to its logical conclusion, however, this drive to separate sound art from music leads theorists like Douglas Kahn (2014) or Caleb Kelly (2017) to reject the notion of sound art outright. Instead, they choose to speak about "sound in the arts", placing the various practices that the term sound art may refer to in the broader context of expanded practice of gallery art in the late twentieth century. To Kelly (2017), this is simply because there is always some sound in the gallery, accompanying the exhibition, and therefore there is no need to invent a separate term for sounding gallery practices. Kahn's (2014) position is more ideological: he argues against the "musicalisation" of sound—stripping it of its discursive context—which he accuses composers like John Cage of, championing instead gallery sound artists working in the poststructuralist and (post)conceptualist paradigms. Kahn's argument is similar to that of Seth Kim-Cohen (2009, xv–xxiv), who calls for "non-cochlear sonic art" that would interrogate the social, political and discursive grounds of auditory culture instead of "letting sounds be themselves".

While acknowledging the sociality of sound in one way or another, the definitions discussed above tend to de-emphasise participation, subsuming it into either spatiality, in case of LaBelle and Ouzounian, or discourse, in case of Kahn and Kim-Cohen. I am additionally suspicious of the theories of "sound in the arts" as they essentially reassert the hegemony of the mainstream histories and theories of contemporary art, discarding the idiosyncratic discourse of sound art.

In his article "Musicophobia, or sound art and the demands of art theory", Brian Kane (2013) juxtaposes Voegelin's and Kim-Cohen's approaches. He notes that for all their disagreements—one arguing in favour of "sounds in themselves", the other, against—they find a common ground in being "musicophobic". In fervently distancing themselves from music, Kane argues, and basing their notions of sound and sound art on this othering, both theorists end up short, failing to account for the immutable connection between the materiality of sound and its sociality.

Attempts to reconcile sound art with music have been made as well. Mirroring Voegelin's argument, Leigh Landy (2017) points out that nothing stops the listener from approaching sound artworks as music. At the same time, the growing corpus of music sociology and anthropology research reveals that music as well supports a wide variety of listenings (DeNora 2000, 2003; Hennion 2015). In a later text, Voegelin (2016, n.p.) herself argues that "[t]here is something we cannot hear, that remains inaudible in the works we listen to if we do not hear them within the holistic and plural complexity of influences and histories" of sound and music; it is only by "[c]onsidering sound art in relation to music" that sound's materiality and conceptuality can be reconciled.

The issues of participation have been discussed in musicological texts for a surprisingly longer time than in sound art ones, beginning with Umberto Eco's (1989) classic *The Open Work*, inspired by the practices of aleatoric music. In *Music as Social Life*, ethnomusicologist Thomas Turino (2008) argues that instead of being a monolithic phenomenon, music is a composite of four distinct, if interrelated, practices: presentational performance, participatory performance, hi-fidelity audio (pop music and concert recordings) and studio audio art (electronic or "tape" music). Presentational performance refers to the traditional setup of concert music, participatory performance, to phenomena like community singing, jam sessions or disco nights. Turino argues that there exists a principal difference between the two: a participatory performance does not distinguish between artists and audience (though may differentiate between various roles and skill levels of the participants) and is judged on the quality of participation rather than the quality of sonic product.

Several issues stop me from considering participatory sound art a form of participatory music performance as defined by Turino. First, Turino's notion of participatory performance does not differentiate between collective soundmaking and merely dancing to music—both are considered a form of musical participation. At the same time, it does exclude the kind of solitary participation through listening that Voegelin talks about. Finally, participatory music practices, according to Turino, are entrenched in traditions and rely on the participants' familiarity with the sonic features, reaffirming the participants' group identity and invoking a sense of sameness. Participatory sound art, on the contrary, emphasises experimental and exploratory soundmaking and listening, troubling the identities and sonic habits.

To sum it up, sound art—at least when approached from the perspective of sociality and participation—resists both the attempts to separate it from music and the attempts to bring it into the musical fold. My answer to this conundrum in this book is to consider the music-sound art divide across two planes: ontological and presentational. Given the constant expanding and redefining of the musical field, it is hard to argue in favour of sound art's ontological separateness without making a strawman out of music. However, there is a tactical advantage in emphasising the presentational difference.

In an earlier article, I have defined sound art as a category encompassing "any sound-based artworks that happen outside of musical institutions and do not conform to the traditional musical presentation formats such as concert performance or recording" (Keylin 2020, 100). The additional benefit of this approach is that it allows to include experimental sonic practices of participatory culture (that I discuss in parts of Chaps. 2 and 4) in the continuum of sound art. However, due to the limited scope of this book, it focuses primarily on works that are institutionally framed as art in one way or another—by being presented in art spaces, or curated, produced, or funded by art- and culture-focused bodies.

My aim in distancing from the institutional contexts and traditions of music is to avoid the tenets of Western music theory and emphasise sound art's connection to a broader range of non-musical sonic practices, whether participatory or not—sound design, Foley art, radio art etc. On the other hand, my working definition purposefully does not specify in any way the kinds of sound that sound artworks are based on—indeed, the works discussed in this book may employ noises, everyday sounds, vocalising and spoken word as their sonic material, as well as conventionally musical sounds, and even music recordings. In line with the pragmatist position, my focus in on how sounds are used (i.e., differently from how they are typically used in music) rather than what they are.

Furthermore, underscoring the presentational difference, I also strive to avoid, wherever possible, describing the actors in participatory sound art works in terms of hierarchy of concert music roles of composers, performers or audience. The latter is particularly important to consider with regard to participation, as its whole point is to upset the artist-audience dichotomy. The next stage, then, is to define how exactly this upsetting occurs.

1.3 Participation, Interactivity, Collaboration

Unlike sound art, participatory art is not strictly a separate art form, but rather a set of practices happening across different arts and even non-artistic media. As such, it is defined not against other art forms, but against practices that could be considered non-participation. However, much like with sound art, the definitions are extremely contested and the theorists' positions run the gamut from considering all forms of audience experience participatory (White 2013) to using very narrow and rigid criteria, e.g., only considering participatory art "where people constitute the central artistic medium and material" (Bishop 2012, 1–2).

Most often, a spectrum of interactivity, participation and collaboration emerges in the works of different theorists to denote different artist-participant relationships [although parts of this continuum can be omitted—e.g., Grant Kester (2011) does not distinguish between interactivity and participation, while Claire Bishop (2012), between participation and collaboration]. Typically, this refers to the degree of creative agency afforded to the participants. For example, Anna Dezeuze (2010, 6) in the introduction to *The "Do-it-Yourself" Artwork* considers a distinction (adopted from Beryl Graham's essay in the same volume) between interactive artworks, where "content is generated by the artist and arranged by the participants", participatory artworks, where, conversely, "content is generated by the participants and curated by the artist", and collaboration, that "aims at erasing altogether the difference between producers and recipients". On the other hand, Claire Bishop (2006, 10) bases her definition mainly on the degree of collectivity, distinguishing between participatory art, which engages its audience as a group and "appropriate[s] social forms as a way to bring art closer to everyday life", and interactive art, which implies a one-on-one interaction between the individual viewer and the artwork.

Sound art tends to complicate such definitions. On the one hand, most of the artworks discussed in the following chapters have the participants produce their own sonic content in one way or another: by using their voices, playing sound sculptures, supplying their audio recordings etc. On the other hand, it does not make sense to exclude the creative agency of listening that Voegelin (2010) talks about, particularly in the context of sound installations, as it also represents an upsetting of the typical concert listening situation. Neither does the solitary-collective distinction work. While one-on-one interaction is possible for many of participatory sound artworks, sound, as LaBelle (2015) notes, has a tendency to spread, resonate and stipulate in others a response in kind.

This is not a situation entirely unique to sound art. Dezeuze (2010, 12), after considering the various definitions of participation and its others, rejects rigid distinctions altogether, opting instead to consider participation a continuum, "spanning the two extremes of constraint and openness". My approach in this book is similar. As my definition of sound art is apophatically set against the institutions and presentational formats of music, I am similarly considering as participatory any sound artwork that reverses, rejects or questions, in any way or degree, the linear listening protocols implied in the practices of concert performance and audio playback. While my main interest lies with the practices that cast the audience as sound producers, soundmaking exists in a continuum with listening, and therefore "active" listening practices also belong to the continuum of participation. This continuum is thus bounded by the extremes of linear, passive listening and free-for-all unrestricted soundmaking, though arguably neither of these occurs in a pure form in real-world practices. At the same time, while I aim to address this continuum as a whole, my main focus lies with practices positioned further away from the linear listening, and particularly those that invite participatory soundmaking.

Furthermore, the continuum of participation may be graduated by many different criteria, stratifying the field of participatory sound art. Dezeuze (2010, 7) suggests to explore the temporality of participatory artworks, some of which "privilege the experience of here and now (whether [...] individual or collective, reversible or not), whereas others privilege a cumulative experience over a fixed duration [...] which involves more than one participant maintaining or transforming the material existence of the work". Given sound's ephemeral and real-time character, participatory sound artworks tend to favour the former end of this scale, lacking the materiality to be permanently altered. Asynchronous participation is not impossible, however. For example, Pedro Rebelo and Rodrigo Cicchelli Velloso (2018) in their chapter in *The Routledge Research Companion to Electronic Music* discuss their workshop practices that involved the participants collecting filed recordings over a period of time, culminating in exhibitions or performances using the material gathered.

Participatory literature scholar Scott Rettberg (2011) offers another salient parameter to consider: the degree to which the participants are aware of their contribution to the project and how it will be used. A similar notion can be found in Gareth White's (2013) characterising of the contract of participation as either overt, implicit or covert. The notion of unwitting participation is particularly important here as it reframes the artworks that explore ready-made sounds—soundwalks in particular—as participatory, as the producers of these ready-made sounds become the unwitting participants.

The considerations above raise the question of whether participatory sound art can indeed be understood as a subcategory of sound art—in other words, whether non-participatory sound art exists at all. This question is largely inherent to the discussion of participatory art of any kind—it is hardly possible to imagine an art form that completely excludes audience participation. My goal in referring to sound artworks as participatory is to emphasise the importance of participation to the discussion at hand rather than to construe a specific genre of participatory sound art against its linear other. Like much of the theoretical and epistemological framework of this book, this approach is indebted to Dewey (1980 [1934]) who defined individual art forms not as rigid categories describing finite corpora but as poles of attraction in the continuous field of art.

References

Agamben, Giorgio. 1993. Notes on gesture. In *Infancy and history: Essays on the destruction of experience*, 135–140. London: Verso Books.

———. 1999. Kommerell, or on gesture. In *Potentialities: Collected essays in philosophy*, ed. Daniel Heller-Roazen, 77–85. Stanford: Stanford University Press.

Bala, Sruti. 2018. *The gestures of participatory art*. Manchester: Manchester University Press.

Baschet, François, and Bernard Baschet. 1987. Sound sculpture: Sounds, shapes, public participation, education. *Leonardo* 20: 107–114.

Bishop, Claire, ed. 2006. *Participation*. London: Whitechapel.
———. 2012. *Artificial hells: Participatory art and the politics of spectatorship*. London: Verso Books.
Born, Georgina. 2005. On musical mediation: Ontology, technology and creativity. *Twentieth-Century Music* 2: 7–36. https://doi.org/10.1017/S147857220500023X.
Cox, Christoph. 2009. Sound art and the sonic unconscious. *Organised Sound* 14: 19.
———. 2018. *Sonic flux: Sound, art and metaphysics. Sonic Flux*. Chicago: University of Chicago Press.
Czolbe, Fabian. 2014. Klangkunst goes mobile. In *Proceedings of the Electroacoustic Music Studies Network Conference "Electroacoustic Music Beyond Performance."* Berlin.
DeNora, Tia. 2000. *Music in everyday life*. Cambridge: Cambridge University Press.
———. 2003. *After Adorno: Rethinking music sociology*. Cambridge: Cambridge University Press.
Dewey, John. 1930 [1916]. *Democracy and education: An introduction to the philosophy of education*. New York: The Macmillan Company.
———. 1980 [1934]. *Art as experience*. New York: Perigee Books.
Dezeuze, Anna. 2010. An introduction to the 'do-it-yourself' artwork. In *The "do-it-yourself" artwork: Participation from fluxus to new media*, ed. Anna Dezeuze, 1–21. Manchester: Manchester University Press.
Dinkla, Söke. 1996. From participation to interaction: Toward the origins of interactive art. In *Clicking in: Hot links to a digital culture*, ed. Lynn Hershman Leeson, 279–290. Seattle: Bay Press.
Eco, Umberto. 1989. *The open work*. Translated by Anna Cancogni. Cambridge, MA: Harvard University Press.
Engström, Andreas, and Åsa Stjerna. 2009. Sound art or Klangkunst? A reading of the German and English literature on sound art. *Organised Sound* 14: 11–18. Cambridge University Press. https://doi.org/10.1017/S13557718090 0003X.
Gibson, James Jerome. 1979. *The ecological approach to visual perception*. Boston, MA: Houghton Mifflin.
Glaveanu, Vlad Petre. 2018. Creativity in perspective: A sociocultural and critical account. *Journal of Constructivist Psychology* 31: 118–129. Routledge. https://doi.org/10.1080/10720537.2016.1271376.
Heinrich, Falk. 2014. *Performing beauty in participatory art and culture*. Abingdon: Routledge.
Hennion, Antoine. 2015. *The passion for music: A sociology of mediation*. Farnham: Ashgate.
Jackson, Shannon. 2011. *Social works: Performing art, supporting publics*. Abingdon: Routledge.
Kahn, Douglas. 2014. Sound art, art, music. *Tacet* 3: 329–347.

Kane, Brian. 2013. Musicophobia, or sound art and the demands of art theory. *Nonsite.Org*: 1–20.
Kelly, Caleb. 2017. *Gallery sound*. New York and London: Bloomsbury.
Kester, Grant. 2004. *Conversation pieces: Community and communication in modern art*. Berkeley, CA: University of California Press.
———. 2011. *The one and the many: Contemporary collaborative art in a global context*. Durham, NC: Duke University Press.
Keylin, Vadim. 2015. Corporeality of music and sound sculpture. *Organised Sound* 20: 182–190. Cambridge University Press. https://doi.org/10.1017/S1355771815000060.
———. 2020. Crash, boom, bang: Affordances for participation in sound art. *SoundEffects* 9: 98–115. https://doi.org/10.7146/se.v9i1.118243.
———. 2021. Sound acts: Towards a sonic pragmatism. *Sound Studies* 7: 83–99. Routledge. https://doi.org/10.1080/20551940.2020.1857622.
Kim-Cohen, Seth. 2009. *In the blink of an ear: Toward a non-cochlear sonic art*. New York and London: Continuum.
Krogh Groth, Sanne, and Holger Schulze. 2020. Sound art: The first 100 years of an aggressively expanding art form. In *The Bloomsbury handbook of sound art*, ed. Sanne Krogh Groth and Holger Schulze, 1–18. London: Bloomsbury.
LaBelle, Brandon. 2015. *Background noise: Perspectives on sound art*. 2nd ed. New York: Bloomsbury.
Landy, Leigh. 2017. But is it (also) music. In *Routledge companion to sounding art*, ed. Marcel Cobussen, Vincent Meelberg, and Barry Truax. eBook edition. Routledge.
Latour, Bruno. 1994. On technical mediation. *Common Knowledge* 3: 29–64.
———. 2004. Why has critique run out of steam? From matters of fact to matters of concern. *Critical Inquiry* 30: 225–248. https://doi.org/10.1086/421123.
———. 2005. *Reassembling the social: An introduction to actor-network-theory*. Oxford: Oxford University Press.
Licht, Alan. 2007. *Sound art: Beyond music, between categories*. New York: Rizzoli; Har/Com edition.
———. 2019. *Sound art revisited*. New York and London: Bloomsbury.
Mauss, Marcel. 1973 [1935]. Techniques of the body. *Economy and Society* 2: 70–88.
Mead, George Herbert. 1938. *The philosophy of the act*. Chicago: University of Chicago Press.
———. 1972 [1934]. *Mind, self and society: From the standpoint of a social behaviorist*. Chicago: University of Chicago Press.
Motte-Haber, Helga de la. 1996. Klangkunst—eine neue Gattung? In *Klangkunst*, ed. Akademie der Künste Berlin, 12–18. Munich: Prestel.
———, ed. 1999. *Klangkunst: Tönende Objekte und klingende Räume*. Laaber: Laaber-Verlag.

Neuhaus, Max. 1994. The broadcast works and audium. In *Zeitgleich: The symposium, the seminar, the exhibition*. Vienna: Triton.

Neuhaus, Max, and Gregory des Jardins, eds. 1994. *Max Neuhaus: Sound works. Vol. 1: Inscription*. Ostfildern: Cantz.

Noland, Carrie. 2010. *Agency and embodiment: Performing gestures/producing culture*. Cambridge, MA: Harvard University Press.

Ouzounian, Gascia. 2008. *Sound art and spatial practices: Situating sound installation art since 1958*. PhD dissertation, UC San Diego.

———. 2013. Sound installation art. In *Music, sound and space*, ed. Georgina Born, 73–89. Cambridge: Cambridge University Press.

Pierce, Charles Sanders. 1935. In *The collected papers of Charles Sanders Pierce. Vol. V*, ed. Charles Hartshorne and Paul Weiss. Cambridge, MA: Harvard University Press.

Rebelo, Pedro, and Rodrigo Cicchelli Velloso. 2018. Participatory sonic arts: The Som de Maré project—Towards a socially engaged art of sound in the everyday. In *The Routledge research companion to electronic music—Reaching out with technology*, ed. Simon Emmerson, 137–155. Abingdon: Routledge.

Rettberg, Scott. 2011. All together now: Hypertext, collective narratives, and online collective knowledge communities. In *New narratives: Stories and storytelling in the digital age*, ed. Ruth Page and Thomas Bronwen, 187–204. Lincoln, NE: University of Nebraska Press.

Turino, Thomas. 2008. *Music as social life: The politics of participation*. Chicago: University of Chicago Press.

Voegelin, Salomé. 2010. *Listening to noise and silence: Toward a philosophy of sound art*. New York and London: Continuum.

———. 2016. Historical interest: A pragmatic provocation for a continuum of sound. In *Colloquium: Sound art and music*, ed. Thomas Gardner and Salomé Voegelin. eBook edition. John Hunt Publishing.

Vogel, Peter. 1996. *Peter Vogel: Interaktive Objekte, eine Retrospektive*. Mainz: Skulpturenmuseum Glaskasten.

White, Gareth. 2013. *Audience participation in theatre: Aesthetics of the invitation*. New York: Palgrave Macmillan.

Wilson, Stephen. 2002. *Information arts: Intersections of art, science, and technology*. Cambridge, MA: MIT Press.

CHAPTER 2

Histories

Abstract This chapter demonstrates how participatory sensibilities have been the core aspect of sound art since its very inception. It traces the histories of sound art and participatory art—as both artistic practices and theoretical concepts—from their common beginnings in the Avantgarde interpretations of the *Gesamtkunstwerk*, through their divergence in late twentieth century as both art forms become institutionally established, to recombination of sound and participation in interactive media art and participatory culture. The chapter follows the reciprocal relationships between the development of the practices of sound art and participatory art and the broader theoretical fields of sound studies and participation studies, identifying the premises and the consequences of their discursive split along the aesthetics/politics and perception/production lines.

Keywords Historical Avantgarde · Post-war Avantgarde · Digital culture · Sound sculpture · Sound installation · Relational aesthetics

2.1 Sound, Participation and *Gesamtkunstwerk*

As I suggest in the introduction, academic conceptualisations of participatory art and sound art are rather divergent. However, the same cannot be said about the practices themselves. In this chapter I will briefly discuss the histories of sound art and participatory art in order to show, first, how they developed in parallel and often in connection to each other, and second, how and why their discourses started to diverge. This will be followed by a brief discussion of interactive and participatory sonic practices that emerged independently in digital culture and their intersections with participatory sound art. The goal of this chapter is not to offer a comprehensive historical account, but rather to highlight the developments that reveal the connections between sound art and participatory practices. For the same reason, my scope is also mostly limited to the Western art history of the twentieth century.

The origins of both sound art and participatory art in the Western context can be traced to Richard Wagner's concept of the *Gesamtkunstwerk*. While it is easy to see how the idea of bringing all artistic disciplines together in a united artwork would herald the intermediality of sound art, Boris Groys (2008) in his article "A genealogy of participatory art" highlights a different aspect of Wagner's project. Reading Wagner's manifesto "The art-work of the future", Groys emphasises the composer's call for "the passing over of Egoism into Communism" and his proclamation that "all great inventions are the People's deed; whereas the devisings of the intellect are but the exploitations, the derivatives [...] of the great invention of the Folk" (as quoted in Groys 2008, 21–23). According to Groys, then, the unity of artistic media in a *Gesamtkunstwerk* is not an end in itself but serves predominantly as a means to achieve a social unity and the dissolution of this individual creativity in the creativity of the people. I want to stress the connection drawn here between the materiality of art (the intermedial unity of different arts) and its sociality (the unity of people), which somehow got lost along the way in the sound art and participatory art discourses, and which this book aims to re-establish.

Much like they can be traced to the same source, sound and participation gain prominence during the same three distinct periods in the twentieth-century art history: the historical Avantgarde (1910s to 1920s), the Post-war Avantgarde (mid-1950s to mid-1970s) and the current period of expansion of the two art forms, whose starting point can be roughly placed in late 1980s.[1] The three periods also show a progression

---

[1] I am mostly following Claire Bishop's (2012) periodisation of participatory art here, associating the developments in art to major events in Western history: The First World War and October Revolution (historical Avantgarde), The Second World War and 1968 protests (post-war Avantgarde) and end of Cold War and dissolution of the Soviet Union (current period).

of the two discourses diverging: where in historical Avantgarde sound works and participatory works were largely created by the same art groups, if not necessarily the same people within those art groups, in Post-war Avantgarde they can be seen as responses to the same themes, while the current period all connection seems to be lost. The final section of this chapter concerns sound and participation in digital culture, which can be understood both as a period in itself, the digital age, and as a cultural trend that developed from the mid-twentieth century in parallel to sound art and participatory art.

2.2 Sound and Participation in Historical Avantgarde

For historical Avantgarde art both sound and participation become manifestations of the general impulse to merge art and everyday life. Italian Futurist painter and composer Luigi Russolo (1986 [1913], 25) wrote in his manifesto *The Art of Noises*: "we delight much more in combining in our thoughts the noises of trams, of automobile engines, of carriages and brawling crowds, than in hearing again the 'Eroica' or the 'Pastorale'".

For Russolo, this delight led to his invention of the *Intonarumori*, noise instruments that would mimic industrial sounds. Similarly, Dadaists have produced a number of noisy objects, such as Duchamp's *A Bruit Secret* (1916) or Man Ray's *Indestructible Object* (1923/58). Both groups also used noise as a means of provoking their audiences—a phenomenon Claire Bishop (2012, Chap. 2) considers the origin of "antagonistic" participation. As Bishop (2012, 45–46) argues, despite their antagonising the public, the Avantgarde provocations were "spectator*philic*" as they "were not designed to negate the presence of the audience, but to exaggerate it, to make it visible to itself, to stir it up, halt complacency, and cultivate confidence rather than docile respect". Similarly, recent New Materialist studies of noise (Hainge 2013; Thompson 2017) have conceptualised it not as a nuisance or an environmental hazard but as a productive relational force that suffuses the everyday life of both humans and non-humans. From that perspective, the use of noise in Futurist and Dadaist performances can similarly be heard as a means of engaging the public into the creative relationship through the affective mediation of noise.

At the same time, the idea of noise as participatory music of the everyday received a number of much more straightforward realisations in early

Soviet art. The most famous of those—and one of the few works that is actually included in both participatory art and sound art canons—is Arseny Avraamov's *Symphony of Industrial Horns*[2] (e.g., Bishop 2012; Licht 2019). This monumental performance of noise music involved thousands of volunteers spread across a whole city and playing instruments such as factory sirens, airplanes, cannons, machine guns etc. On a smaller scale, and somewhat less known in the West, was the noise orchestra ("shumork"[3]) movement. Noise orchestras were a facet of Proletkult's cultural policy aimed at fostering the grassroot creativity of the liberated proletariat, and at the same time liberating the arts themselves. This policy has led to the creation of, for example, amateur worker theatres that at one point were numbering in the hundreds or conductor-less music ensembles. In a similar fashion, Boris Yurtsev announced in his 1922 article "The orchestra of things" the creation of music orchestras for each industrial branch composed of the instruments and products typical of the branches. The noise project did not achieve much success within the music field, but for a time found its place in theatre and cinema productions. For example, Eisenstein's play *The Gas Masks* was staged inside the actual facilities of the Moscow Gas Factory, incorporating their soundscapes of industrial work. Eventually, the movement laid the foundation of the Soviet Foley art and sound design for theatre and cinema (see Smirnov 2013; Dudakov-Kashuro 2015). The legacy of these early experiments in participatory music and theatre, however, can be felt throughout both the sound art's and participatory art's later histories: from industrial music to acoustic ecology's aestheticisation of urban sound and from site-specific Happenings to Augusto Boal's Theatre of the Oppressed (1985).

2.3 Sound and Participation in the Post-War Avantgarde

The idea of dissolving the art object in the practices of the everyday returned in the Post-war Avantgarde, reshaped, however, by the rejection of the totalitarian practices and a longing for non-hierarchical structures in

---

[2] The title is typically translated into English as *The Symphony of Sirens*, however this is not entirely correct as Russian *gudok* refers to a steam horn or whistle rather than a siren. I am using the translation suggested by the composer and Avraamov scholar Sergey Khismatov, who has created a number of electronic reconstructions of the *Symphony*.

[3] From Russian *shum* (noise) + *orkestr* (orchestra).

art (see, e.g., Hopkins 2000). Two entangled vectors of this sensibility become particularly important with regard to sound and participation. First, it is the renouncement of artistic authority over the object and the privileging of the viewer's or the listener's perception, manifesting, on the one hand, in aestheticising the everyday, and on the other hand, in the embrace of cybernetics. Second, the very dissatisfaction with the institutions of art as the apparatuses of maintaining entrenched hierarchies found its expression in institutional critique and the search for alternative forms of engaging with the public, for both visual artists and musicians. While the two vectors come from the same source and are essentially inseparable in the post-war art, the typical art-historical narratives show sound art gravitating towards the perceptual aspect, while participatory art, towards the political, leading to the separation of the two practices and their respective discourses in the late twentieth century.

In her essay "'Open work', 'do-it-yourself artwork' and bricolage", Anna Dezeuze (2010) draws a parallel between the pioneering participatory artworks of the Brazilian Neo-Concrete artists and the post-war experimental music, particularly that of John Cage and his circles. According to Dezeuze (2010), what links the two phenomena is the emergence of a new understanding of materiality—not as objecthood but as an embodied experience. Following Merleau-Ponty's (2002 [1981]) phenomenology of perception—a theory which continues to dominate the sound art discourse to this day—both lineages emphasise the agency of the perceiver in creating the (aesthetic) world in her experience.

One way of achieving this was through the explorations of hapticality and processuality of sculpture. Neo-Concretist artists such as Lygia Clark, Hélio Oiticica, Lygia Pape and others created "participatory works made out of everyday materials" where "the tactile and bodily dimension of the participant's experience is paramount as he or she needs to handle or wear objects" (Dezeuze 2010, 47). For example, in Clark's "proposal" (as she referred to her participatory pieces) *Air and Stone* (1966), the spectator was asked to fill a plastic bag with air, place a stone on top and hold it in their hands. While the material components of the work do not have any intrinsic value, it is the act of assembling them that gives the experience an aesthetic dimension.

A very similar understanding of materiality as processual—including, most saliently, the materiality of sound—can be found in the early practice of sound sculpture. With their interactive sound-producing contraptions, artists like Bernard and François Baschet or Harry Bertoia invited the audiences to explore the sonicity of raw materials such as metal, glass or plastic freed from the constraints of established musical forms. Bertoia's works typically featured uniformly arranged metallic rods that would hit one another in chaotic movement when activated by the listener. The Baschets' sculptures retained a closer resemblance to traditional musical instruments, but the sculptors also explored various "interfaces" to make the soundmaking capabilities more intuitive and accessible to non-musicians. They even went to claim "shapes, sounds and public participation" to be principal components of their artworks (Baschet and Baschet 1987).

A particular branch of sound sculpture, represented by, among others, Peter Vogel and Nicolas Schöffer, bridges sound art with emerging interactive media art as well. Following Norbert Wiener's theory of cybernetics as the study of man-machine systems behaviour, Jack Burnham (1968) in his book *Beyond Modern Sculpture* introduced the term "cyborg art". Late 1960s and early 1970s saw the artists create reactive environments built on feedback systems, such as closed-circuit video, or systems that would imitate life-like behaviour. Vogel's sculptures, which he explicitly referred to as cybernetic objects, featured light sensors that activated soundmaking circuitry triggered by the visitors' shadows. However, the relationship between the input and the sonic output was non-linear and relied on previous inputs as well and was affected by a degree of randomness. In this way, Vogel's sculptures operated as independent cybernetic agents with their own behaviours that the listener can interact and communicate with rather than passive objects of artistic expression.

Importantly, this sculptural approach to participation in the 1960s did not necessarily imply solitary one-on-one interactions, both in participatory art and sound art. For example, *A Stitch in Time* (1961) by David Medalla—a Filipino artist close to the Neo-Concrete movement—invited the participants to stitch anything they wanted to the artwork, using the colourful threads hanging nearby, the installation becoming an archive of collective memory. It was also with reference to this materiality that Joseph Beuys (1974) called his brand of politically charged participatory performance "social sculpture". A communal component can be found in sound sculpture as well, for example, in Vogel's *Sound Walls*—several metres long wall-mounted sculptures that could be played by several people at the same time. Another example is the Baschet brother's project for the 1968 Mexico City Olympic Games where the public was invited to assemble and play their own sound sculptures together. In their later work, the Baschets also explicitly engaged with the social issues, harnessing their art for social work and music therapy programmes.

As this side-by-side comparison shows, a dialectic of the experience-centric attitude to form and matter and the materialist attitude to interaction and experience emerge as a common thread uniting early Post-war participatory art and sound sculpture. Breaking with the museum convention of establishing an invisible barrier between the art object and the public, both Neo-Concrete artworks and sound sculptures employ materiality, on the one hand, as an extended experience—not just visual, but haptic and sonic at the same time—and on the other hand, as an "invitation" (White 2013) to act and experience through action.

Dezeuze (2010) observes a further parallel between the Neo-Concretist's explorations of the materiality of physical things and John Cage's project of liberating sound from music. In his *Lecture on Nothing*, Cage (1961, 10) called to "let sounds be themselves rather than vehicles for man-made theories or expression of human sentiments". The notorious silent piece *4′33″* is the utmost expression of this position. In absence of any artist-made sounds, whatever random noises happen to occur in the concert space become the material of the composition. But at the same time, 4′33″ can be read as a participatory piece, since most if not all the random noises that fill the work's silences will inevitably be audience-produced (although the unwitting character of such participation raises questions of the ethics of both aleatoric music and participatory art).

According to Seth Kim-Cohen (2009), Cage's call to "let sounds be themselves" defined much of sound art practice in the coming decades. On the one hand, the aesthetic value of everyday environmental sounds has been explored by the Canadian acoustic ecologists R.M Schafer, Barry Truax, Hildegard Westerkamp in their soundscape compositions and soundwalks, both guided and recorded. On the other hand, the Fluxus movement that emerged directly from Cage's composition class perfected the form of indeterminant and often paradoxical text score. George Brecht's *Drip Music* (1959–62) reads simply: "A source of dripping water and an empty vessel are arranged so that the water falls into the vessel". The short text score emphasises both the aesthetic value to be found in the mundane sound of dripping water and the open character of the work that does not require a professional performer or an intricate composition structure.

Importantly, there is a direct genealogical link between Fluxus events and contemporary participatory art by way of Happenings and performance art of the 1970s and 1980s. Similarly, the potential of indeterminate scores—whether textual or graphic—to be performed by non-musicians led to the emergence of participatory compositional practices. With her *Sonic Meditations*, the American composer Pauline Oliveros (1974) "abandoned composition/performance practice as it is usually established today" focusing instead on poetic textual instructions for solitary and communal listening that would be performable by anyone irrespective of their musical training. In the UK, Cornelius Cardew has founded his Scratch Orchestra on the aesthetic and political principles resembling those of the early Soviet noise orchestras—being open for all and prioritising freedom of expression. To facilitate those ideals the group used graphical scores that could be interpreted by musicians and non-musicians alike.

Such sound art practices, as well as those of sound sculpture, show an interest in consistent questioning of the musical axioms as well as reimagining and liberating sounds, musical instruments or scores from the hierarchical structures of Western art music. However, far from being politically inert, as Kim-Cohen (2009) claims, I would argue that these strategies effectively perform an institutional critique of the established musical paradigms, even if the artists do not necessarily conceptualise them in precisely these terms. Deconstructing the musical whole, foregrounding its individual components and reimagining the relationships between them brings critical attention to the hierarchical structures such as the composer-performers-audience pyramid inherent to Western art music as well as its material conditions. In a parallel movement, some of the practitioners of institutional critique proper in the visual arts employed sound—such as Michael Asher, whose installations often involved introducing continuous tones in lieu of art objects or remodelling the gallery walls themselves in order to emphasise certain aspects of their acoustics. In absence of image, sound questions the assumed neutrality of the exhibition space as a mere background, prompting the audience "to think about [the gallery's] role in the art institution and the types of elements and practices within the culture of exhibition that we take for granted" (Kelly 2017, 28).

The question of the spaces and sites of art production and perception that are interrogated in the works of Asher and other institutional critique projects take a prominent role in the post-war sound art practices as well. So prominent in fact that, as I mentioned in the introduction, many sound art theories and histories put space at the centre of the practice. Here, however, I want to re-read this spatiality as a means of facilitating participation, using the most textbook example of Max Neuhaus' sound installations. Neuhaus is credited with coining the term "sound installation" in 1968, defining it as artworks where sound is distributed in space instead of time—with the explicit goal of making the listener reassemble and experience them in their own time. For example, in *Drive-In Music*, the listener driving a car along a section of a highway would tune in to the radio transmitters installed at the roadside—receiving a different composition depending on their direction, speed, weather conditions and other contingencies. Much like Minimalism and Installation art, Neuhaus' sound installations used space to de-emphasise the art object (the music composition of temporally organised sound) and emphasised the agency of perceiver moving through the space and building their own unique aesthetic experience. Arguably, the listener of *Drive-In Music* experiences the sound of the work not so much as spatially distributed, since all the sounds are coming from the fixed point of their car radio, but rather temporally structured by their movement through that space. Unsurprisingly, the shift to spatiality also marked for Neuhaus (1994, n.p.) a shift "beyond [being a performer] and beyond being a composer, into the idea of being a catalyser of sound activity". In *Broadcast Works* from the same period, he would create a radio composition in real time from the sounds provided by the participants calling the studio.

As this brief overview shows, sound and participation in the art of the 1960s were framed by the same conceptual concerns. Both sound art and participatory or interactive art practices offered ways of moving outside the established institutional borders, rethinking materiality as experience and dissolving the art object (see Lippard 1997 [1973]). The agency of the spectator or listener, variously conceptualised in Umberto Eco's (1989) notion of the open work, or Roland Barthes' (1977) idea of "the death of the author", takes centre stage in both post-war sound art and participatory art, explored through the modes of spatiality, sociality or technological engagement. This connection between the two practices is emphasised by works such as Annea Lockwood's *Piano Transplants* (1968–82)—a series of text scores instructing the performer to variously destroy old pianos with natural forces—that can be interpreted at the same time as musical pieces, Fluxus-like happenings or sound sculptures (Keylin 2015).

At the same time, a disciplinary divide is starting to emerge here, reflected in how these practices are later retrospectively incorporated into either sound art or participatory art histories. While certain figures like

Cage or Schöffer find place in both discourses, no mention of Vogel, Baschets or Neuhaus can be found in the histories of participatory art, and similarly histories of sound art would bracket off the likes of Clark or Beuys.

2.4 Sound and Participation After the Cold War

This disciplinary divide became exacerbated in the 1980s–1990s, when both sound art and participatory art started to receive institutional recognition as art forms in their own right. This process can be traced through a succession of landmark shows. For sound art, those milestones were such exhibitions as *Für Augen und Ohren* (1980) at Akademie der Kunst in Berlin, *Soundings* (1981) in Neuberger Museum in New York, *Sound/Art* (1984) at Sculpture Center also in New York, and festivals like *Sound Art 95* in Hannover, *Sonambiente* in Berlin in 1996, or *SoundCulture* festival that had instances in different cities of the Pacific region throughout the 1990s. Similarly, a number of sound art institutions such as Singuhr gallery emerged in the course of late 1980s and early 1990s. As Alan Licht (2019) notes, these early events and institutions typically saw themselves as meeting points of visual art and music, showing both musicians' and composers' forays into visual and spatially organised work, as well as visual art that referenced or used sound in some ways.

This sensibility is reflected in what could be considered the first monograph on the art form—Helga de la Motte-Haber's *Musik und bildende Kunst: von der Tonmalerei zur Klangskulptur* (1990). In the book, Motte-Haber recounts the history of how certain art practices in the twentieth centuries—such as action painting and kinetic sculpture—have moved towards including movement and duration into a spatial art (*Raumkunst*), while certain musical practices—spatial music, *musique concrète*—introduced space and materiality into a temporal art (*Zeitkunst*). However, the book—much like exhibitions discussed above—stays within this in-between territory, stopping short of conceptualising sound art (German *Klangkunst*) as a new art form in its own right.

The same can be said of Douglas Kahn and Gregory Whitehead's anthology *Wireless Imagination: Sound, Radio and the Avant-Garde* (1992), as well as Kahn's own later text *Noise, Water, Meat: A History of Sound in the Arts* (1999). Both books trace what could be considered prehistory of sound art. They discuss the works of artists and writers that questioned music's exclusive domain over sound but limit their historical scope to early and mid-twentieth century, just before the first forms of sound art emerge. Unlike Motte-Haber, however, this is not just the matter of early discourse formation. As I mentioned in the introduction, Kahn is explicitly critical of notion of sound art, considering it too narrow both aesthetically and historically, opting instead for a broader category of sound in the arts.

These early works are also emblematic of the split in sound art's theorisation between the German and Anglophone scholarship that persisted in the following decades. Where Motte-Haber and the German tradition after her sees (and hears) sound art as interpenetration of music and visual arts, Anglophone literature became more concerned with sound itself as an aesthetic phenomenon operating across genre and art form boundaries (Engström and Stjerna 2009).

It is no surprise then that the first academic volume to offer a comprehensive account of sound art as an art form in its own right—the anthology *Klangkunst: tönende Objekte und klingende Räume* (1999)—came from Germany and was edited by de la Motte-Haber. The book consolidated the concept of sound art as a convergence of spatial and temporal arts; however, it also made an important step towards acknowledging the importance of participation. In the second theoretical chapter of the book, "Autonomie, Intentionalität, Situation. Aspekte eines erweiterten Kunstbegriffs" ("Autonomy, intentionality, situation. Aspects of an expanded concept of art", 1999), Sabine Sanio points to a shift in Postwar aesthetics from artwork to art situation and how it reconfigures the artist-audience relationship. Whereas a musical or a visual work is complete and meant only for contemplation, a sound art situation is fundamentally open; it decentres artistic intent and puts the emphasis on the agency of the listener. Furthermore, a situation is necessarily site-specific and relational, embedded into a variety of spatial, social and semiotic contexts (Doherty 2009). It is rather telling that the term "situation" coming from The Situationist International, another mainstay of participatory art history, applies so readily to sound art, as both practices share the same strong drive to deautomatise the everyday.

From this perspective, the intersecting of the sonic and the visual, the temporal and the spatial in sound art appears not as an end in itself, but as a means of turning a work into a situation, engaging the listener's agency and establishing a relational network. For example, Christina Kubisch, who was trained as a composer, starting in the late 1970s switched from the concert stage to gallery installations "to create spaces where the public could move individually between different sound sources, listen with his/her own inherent time and discover unusual horizons of music" (Installations n.d.). In her works such as *Vogelbaum* ("Bird tree", 1987), she created intricate shapes with audio cables that were not connected to any loudspeakers but could be listened to with special inductive headphones that picked up on electromagnetic emissions from the cables and turned them into sound. Using technology and spatialisation to destabilise the familiar protocols of listening, Kubisch's installations foreground its social performativity, as Seth Kim-Cohen (2009) observes, making the very act of listening the core of the experience—to the extent that the sounds being listened to may even become unimportant. Spatiality, listening and participatory performativity thus become inextricably intertwined as the cables in Kubisch's installations themselves.

Much like the split between sound art and *Klangkunst*, participatory art and its discourse of the 1990s also appear to take different trajectories in the USA and Europe (Bishop 2012). American artists—mostly associated with the New Genre Public Art (NGPA) movement and its ideologues Suzanne Lacy and Suzi Gablik—were concerned with solving concrete social issues through art and participation. In Europe, on the other hand, Nicolas Bourriaud's brand of relational aesthetics with its playful and open-ended approach rose to prominence. Both movements had their key shows: *Culture in Action* (1993) exhibited in the urban spaces of Chicago for NGPA, and *Traffic* (1996, CAPC musée d'art contemporain de Bordeaux) and *Touch: Relational Art from the 1990s to Now* (2002, San Francisco Art Institute) for relational art. More importantly, unlike sound art, both published manifestos of sorts—Bourriaud's eponymous *Relational Aesthetics* (2002 [1998]) and a collection of essays and artist statements *Mapping the Terrain: New Genre Public Art* edited by Suzanne Lacy (1995).

The differences and commonalities between the two tendencies in participatory art of the 1990s can be highlighted by comparing Bourriaud's text with, perhaps, the most programmatic essay in the NGPA collection—Suzi Gablik's (1995) "Connective aesthetics". Both authors claim that in the contemporary situation the modernist model of autonomous art production has become untenable—whether due to growing urbanisation and proximity between actors (Bourriaud), or the realisation of autonomous art's impotence in face of social calamities (Gablik). They both also further the agenda of the dissolution of the art object, although in contrast to the two Avantgardes, it dissolves now into intersubjectivity and relationality rather than everyday life or individual perception. Thus, reimagined as non-autonomous and intersubjective, art becomes a testing ground for new, more horizontal and democratic, modes of sociability and interaction.

Where Gablik and Bourriaud fundamentally differ, however, is in how these new modes of sociability are elaborated. For Bourriaud, the art space has the potential to be an interstice—a blank slate not influenced by capitalistic exchanges and therefore a fertile ground for new emergent communities. Tellingly, he uses a sound art example to illustrate his point—Jens Haaning's *Turkish Jokes* (1994), where jokes in Turkish were broadcast onto a public square, producing "a micro-community, one made up of immigrants brought together by collective laughter, which upsets their exile situation, formed in relation to the work and in it" (Bourriaud 2002 [1998], 17). In Bourriaud's view, thus, the artwork, whether as an object or as a situation, serves as a catalyst—something that precedes and fosters relationality. This finds an important parallel in the conceptualisations of sound (LaBelle 2015) and particularly human voice (Cavarero 2005; Jarman-Ivens 2011) as something inherently social: addressed from one body to another, establishing a relation between them and prompting a response. Sound art thus can be said to have a relational dimension even in cases that do not engage the audiences as co-authors of the work.

Gablik, on the other hand, calls for art's engagement with the existing oppressed communities. Here the artwork becomes the very process of horizontal exchange between the artist and their collaborators, aimed at solving specific social issues. Peculiarly, Gablik uses the metaphor of listening to refer to this mode of artistic production, opposing it to the "disinterested gaze" of vision. Listening to Gablik implies empathy and dialog, decentralising the self and making room for the Other, as the basis of new art and thus mandates participation, blurring the lines between the artist and the audience.

Although Gablik clearly means listening in a discursive or metaphorical sense—as attentiveness to what the other have to say and giving up the artistic agency rather than as sound perception, a certain parallel can be found in the approaches to listening in sound art. Pauline Oliveros' (2005) concept of *Deep Listening*, for example, similarly emphasises relationality and interconnectedness, fostering compassion and understanding through entering the state of intensified attention to one's embeddedness in the world. While described in somewhat spiritualistic and vague language, the Deep Listening practice, as Sharon Stewart (2020) observes, is inseparable from Oliveros' political activism and thus politically charged in itself.

However, the most comparable to the "connective aesthetics" of NGPA is the practice of the sound art collective Ultra-red. Formed in 1994 by the artist Dont Rhine and Marco Larsen, both involved in the Los Angeles ambient scene and ACT UP AIDS activism movement, the art group has conducted numerous "militant sound investigations" (Ultra-red 2008, 1) through listening sessions, conversations and audio recording. Unlike Deep Listening, Ultra-red's (1996, n.p.) practice is explicitly political—in fact, it began "not as electronic musicians doing political music but as political activists accidentally acting as electronic musicians". It grew out of documenting the founders' activism in a needle exchange programme, whose participants understandably declined to be videotaped (Dublon 2018). As an activist group, rather than invite the audience participation, Ultra-red (2008, 3) participate themselves in various communities bound together by "a shared need"—both those they are already part of and those they are invited to conduct their work—engaging in community organising or staging protest actions. For example, one of their earliest projects *Second Nature* (1999) was a mix of recordings made in the Griffith Park, a popular Los Angeles gay cruising spot. In addition to the expected park soundscapes, the record contained the sounds of sex acts, police patrols as well as a protest action organised by the art collective themselves.

In another project, *SILENT/LISTEN* (2005–2006), Ultra-red juxtaposed the Cage's 4′33″ with the ACT UP slogan "Silence=Death". The group organised listening sessions of the iconic silent piece at various organisations working with the AIDS epidemic, followed by a discussion with the participants—medical professionals, community organisers, activists and others. The discussions centred on two questions "What did you hear?" and "When was the last time you were in this space to talk about AIDS?" Each discussion was recorded and used in subsequent sessions, and later released in several albums and sound installations, with the artists further involving the participants in the editing process. SILENT/LISTEN exemplifies Ultra-red's understanding of listening as an iterative, analytical and dialogical activity, where "the silences, sounds, voices and words are shared, listened to over and over, analysed and activated, leaving the issues open and weaving relationships without looking for resolutions" (Carmona 2020, 123). This "pedagogy of the ear" (Ultra-red 2008, 2) was directly informed Paulo Freire's *Pedagogy of the Oppressed* (1970) and thus shares, in another direct parallel to participatory art, a number of methods and goals with Augusto Boal's Theatre of the Oppressed (1985).

The examples briefly discussed above reveal a paradoxical situation: sound art and participatory art practices persist to show a strong connection in the 1990s and beyond, sharing between them number of themes, concepts and approaches. At the same time, their theoretical—both academic and curatorial—reflections take widely divergent paths. While still having as their starting point the dissolution of the art object and the rejection of the work-concept, they take their analyses of the material-social, subject-object unity characteristic of both practices into opposite directions. Sound art becomes the domain of materiality understood either as intermedia exchange (in German literature) or as materiality of sound and sound perception (in Anglophone discourse). Participatory art discourse, on the other hand, places a heavy emphasis on sociality, doing away with the art object altogether and favouring the works "where people constitute the central artistic medium and material" (Bishop 2012, 1–2). The artwork's materiality is relegated to being either a catalyst for sociality (Bourriaud) or, following Conceptual art, merely a signifier of relationality. As the result of this divergence, both the recent participatory sound artworks and the participatory aspects of sound art in general largely remain untheorised, falling through the cracks between the participation and sound discourses.

2.5 Interactive Audio and Digital Culture

As I discussed in the section on Post-war Avantgarde, the artists' fascination with new media and technologies has driven much of sound and participatory work in the 1960s. This fascination, however, coalesced over the course of the following decades into a separate artform, most commonly known as media art (see Grau 2007), although this term has become somewhat contested. Histories of media art, and particularly its subgenre of interactive art, often include early cybernetic sound works, such as Nicolas Schöffer's sculptures, and the artists of Cage's circle (Dinkla 1996).

This is hardly surprising since audiovisuality (or, more generally, multimodality) and interactivity are known to be the defining traits of new media per se (see Bolter and Grusin 1999). The concept of immersion is furthermore important, being opposed to the contemplative modalities of old media (see Dyson 2009). As sound is an immersive medium par excellence, it has become an important aspect to virtual reality (VR) works in particular. For example, Maurice Benayoun's VR installation *Wild Skin* not only placed the viewer in the middle of a war zone landscape but immersed them into a soundscape of gunfire as well. In turn, sound art in the twenty-first century has been influenced by growing popularity of virtual and augmented reality as well, as I will discuss in Chap. 4.

Sound is so omnipresent in contemporary media and post-media art that some theorists felt the need to distinguish between sound art proper and works that only use sound without making it the core of the experience (e.g., Maes and Leman 2017). For others, like Douglas Kahn (1999, 2014) or Caleb Kelly (2017), this is further proof that sound art does not make sense as a separate category.

Descending from audiovisual media, new media artworks tend to approach sound, interactive or not, as a companion to the image—a soundtrack of sorts that the listener merely accesses. As this book focuses on participatory creative soundmaking, most of the media art proper is beyond the scope of my discussion. However, developments in new media outside of the immediate art context—particularly, the internet—have drastically reimagined participatory sonic practices in the twenty-first century.

In his manifesto "I Am Looking for a Field Character", Joseph Beuys (1974) famously proclaimed that "every human being is an artist". Much of participatory art was concerned with creating a space where the layperson could channel their inherent creativity denied to them by their everyday life. Through the emergence of the so-called web 2.0—a set of technologies allowing the regular user an easy way to express themselves on the internet—around the turn of the century, a similar space was established, however one not governed by art's institutions and protocols. Henry Jenkins (2006) has described the online culture as a whole as participatory in the sense that it does not distinguish between creators and audiences: every user can play both roles in different contexts.

Participatory culture can be said to represent the same avant-gardist drive to dissolve the boundaries between art and everyday that runs through the histories of sound art and participatory art. In his Instagram essay "Repetition mindset", artist Brad Troemel (2020) ironically comments on how meme culture has realised the Avantgarde aspirations that institutionalised art failed to achieve. Unlike art, memes, according to Troemel, have successfully dematerialised the art object and represent the "aesthetic forefront of visual culture" that is "created and appreciated by anyone". The same largely applies to sound. Already in 2003, Alvaro Barbosa (2003, 53–54) claimed that the internet should be regarded as a new type of "acoustic community" (Barry Truax's term—see Truax 1984, chap. 5) with its own collectively created soundscape.

The effect of participatory culture on sound art was twofold. On the one hand, it led institutionally established artists to engage with online platforms as means of facilitating collective and participatory performances. For example, *Auracle* was an online sound installation launched in 2004 by Max Neuhaus together with Fellows of Akademie Schloss Solitude Jason Freeman, C. Ramakrishnan and Kristjan Varnik. The authors described this project as "a voice-controlled, networked sound instrument" (Freeman et al. 2005, 221–222). *Auracle* allowed its users, wherever they were located, to play a software synthesiser together over the internet using their voices as a control mechanism. The application analysed the vocal input, translated it into control data and then distributed this data to all the users connected to a current session. The received data in turn was used to define the parameters of sound synthesis. Neuhaus and his collaborators thus classified *Auracle*, after Barbosa, as a "shared sonic environment"—"openly shared [space, where] members of the online community can participate in a public event by manipulating or transforming sounds and musical structures" (Barbosa 2003, 57).

While projects like *Auracle* employ the participatory capabilities of online platforms, they remain technological extensions of existing participatory art models. In a sense, they are top-down: initiated by an institutionally supported artist and inscribed in this artist's portfolio as *their* work. Participatory culture, however, has also created a space for bottom-up sonic practices. Most of these practices—like, e.g., soundcloud rap—conform to traditional ideas of music; however, because of inherently playful character of participatory culture, some of them venture into more experimental territories.

One of the earliest and the most instructive cases is the Microsound online community that formed already in the late 1990s. It emerged around the practice of granular synthesis—a method of audio design through combining multitudes of sound "grains" of minuscule duration into larger sonic textures. While traditionally the domain of experimental and academic electronic music, granular synthesis spread online, on the one hand, through pirated and later open-source software that gave the creators outside of academic institutions access to relevant tools. On the other hand, the Microsound mailing list, established in 1999, served as a discussion forum for ideas exchange and informal mentorship, bringing the community together. Together these two mechanisms provided a way for amateur creators to partake in an experimental music and sound art practice on equal footing with professional artists (see Born and Haworth 2017).

Other internet musics function in a manner closer to conceptual art than to music proper. For example, Vaporwave pieces are made from haphazardly processed samples, often of low quality to begin with, of "elevator music" of late 1980s and 1990s. Rather than providing pleasant listening experiences, Vaporwave is meant to be appreciated as an ironic "uncreative" (see Goldsmith 2011) act. In this regard, it comes closer to being a meme than a piece of music proper (Born and Haworth 2017). In recent years, a wide variety of sonic memes—such as autotuned news clips or experiments with rubber chicken—has emerged that even forgo any pretence of being music pieces. I will discuss these practices in more detail in Chap. 4.

The playfulness of participatory culture finds a parallel—and an extension—in another playful digital media: video games. This is particularly noticeable in the case of circuit-bending—the practice of hacking old gaming hardware to use is as a musical instrument or a sound sculpture. Circuit-bending is characterised by the same core traits as online sonic practices—the ethos of experimentation reinforced by lacking or incomplete knowledge of how the hardware operates and the low entrance barrier due to cheap costs of hardware—and exhibits a similar technological nostalgia to Vaporwave (see Collins 2013, Chap. 4). As in case of Microsound, the online community serves as a bridge between amateur creators and a somewhat professionalised scene.

Finally, the emergence of social media in the past decade provided the artists with massive amounts of data, which could be mined and sonified. The most famous example of such projects, *#tweetscapes*, was an online audiovisual installation by Anselm Nehls and Tarik Barri that ran from 2012 to 2015. It produced a real-time sonification of the activities in the German Twitter segment. Each tweet posted by the users, as long as it could be identified as coming from Germany, caused a distinct sonic and visual event. The characteristics of sound and visual effects were determined by a complex algorithm taking into account the content of the tweet, its hashtags, geotags, number of retweets etc. The artists categorised it as both a sonification project—"a representation of data through sound"—and "a never-ending interactive composition, performed 24/7 by Germany's Twitter users" (Nehls and Barri 2012).

#tweetscapes points to the impossibility of distinguishing between aesthetic and everyday activities in digital culture. Some—likely, most—of the

participants may not have intended for their posts to be fed into the sound installations, if they were even aware of its existence. The ethics of such appropriation of participation can be also put into question, as *#tweetscapes* collect and the data produced by Twitter users and present it to the artwork's audience without the producers' consent.

As this brief survey shows, contemporary sound art is deeply entangled in the circuits of digital culture, and particularly participatory culture. Much like with participatory art throughout the twentieth century, this relationship is reciprocal: not only has internet and other digital media become another tool in a sound artist's toolbox, but sonic experimentation suffuses the grassroots online practices as well. This arguably makes it necessary to extend the understanding of participatory sound art beyond the boundaries of art institution and artwork per se.

References

Barbosa, Álvaro. 2003. Displaced soundscapes: A survey of network systems for music and sonic art creation. *Leonardo Music Journal* 13: 53–59.
Barthes, Roland. 1977. The death of the author. In *Image, music, text*. Translated by Stephen Heath. London: Fontana Press.
Baschet, François, and Bernard Baschet. 1987. Sound sculpture: Sounds, shapes, public participation, education. *Leonardo* 20: 107–114.
Beuys, Joseph. 1974. I am searching for field character. In *Art into society, society into art: Seven German artists*, ed. Caroline Tisdall, 48. London: Institute of Contemporary Art.
Bishop, Claire. 2012. *Artificial hells: Participatory art and the politics of spectatorship*. London: Verso Books.
Boal, Augusto. 1985. *Theatre of the oppressed*. New York: Theatre Communications Group.
Bolter, Jay David, and Richard Grusin. 1999. *Remediation: Understanding new media*. Cambridge, MA: MIT Press.
Born, Georgina, and Christopher Haworth. 2017. From microsound to vaporwave: Internet-mediated musics, online methods, and genre. *Music and Letters* 98: 601–647.
Bourriaud, Nicolas. 2002 [1998]. *Relational aesthetics*. Translated by Simon Pleasance and Fronza Woods. Dijon: Les Presses du réel.
Burnham, Jack. 1968. *Beyond modern sculpture: The effects of science and technology on the sculpture of this century*. New York: G. Braziller.
Cage, John. 1961. *Silence: Lectures and writings*. Middletown, CT: Wesleyan University Press.

Carmona, Susana Jiménez. 2020. Silences and policies in the shared listening: Ultra-red and Escuchatorio. *SoundEffects—An Interdisciplinary Journal of Sound and Sound Experience* 9: 116–131. https://doi.org/10.7146/se.v9i1.112931.

Cavarero, Adriana. 2005. *For more than one voice: Toward a philosophy of vocal expression*. Stanford, CA: Stanford University Press.

Collins, Karen. 2013. *Playing with sound: A theory of interacting with sound and music in video games*. Cambridge, MA: MIT Press.

Dezeuze, Anna. 2010. 'Open work', 'do-it-yourself artwork' and bricolage. In *The "do-it-yourself" artwork: Participation from Fluxus to new media*, ed. Anna Dezeuze. Manchester: Manchester University Press.

Dinkla, Söke. 1996. From participation to interaction: Toward the origins of interactive art. In *Clicking in: Hot links to a digital culture*, ed. Lynn Hershman Leeson, 279–290. Seattle: Bay Press.

Doherty, Claire. 2009. *Situation*. Cambridge, MA: MIT Press.

Dublon, Amalle. 2018. Second nature/2nd nature. *GLQ: A Journal of Lesbian and Gay Studies* 24: 509–516. https://doi.org/10.1215/10642684-6957856.

Dudakov-Kashuro, Konstantin. 2015. Musica ex machina: At the origins of sound industrialization [Musica ex machina: u istokove industrializacii zvuka]. *Iskusstvo* 2 (593): 24–35.

Dyson, Frances. 2009. *Sounding new media: Immersion and embodiment in the arts and culture*. Berkeley, CA: University of California Press.

Eco, Umberto. 1989. *The open work*. Translated by Anna Cancogni. Cambridge, MA: Harvard University Press.

Engström, Andreas, and Åsa Stjerna. 2009. Sound art or Klangkunst? A reading of the German and English literature on sound art. *Organised Sound* 14: 11–18. Cambridge University Press. https://doi.org/10.1017/S135577180900003X.

Freeman, Jason, C. Kristjan Varnik, Max Neuhaus Ramakrishnan, Phil Burk, and David Birchfield. 2005. Auracle: A voice-controlled, networked sound instrument. *Organised Sound* 10: 221–231.

Freire, Paulo. 1970. *Pedagogy of the oppressed*. New York: Seabury Press.

Gablik, Suzi. 1995. Connective aesthetics: Art after individualism. In *Mapping the terrain: New genre public art*, ed. Suzanne Lacy, 88–93. Seattle: Bay Press.

Goldsmith, Kenneth. 2011. *Uncreative writing: Managing language in the digital age*. New York: Columbia University Press.

Grau, Oliver. 2007. *MediaArtHistories*. Cambridge, MA: MIT Press.

Groys, Boris. 2008. A genealogy of participatory art. In *The art of participation: 1950 to now*, ed. San Francisco Museum of Modern Art, 18–31. London: Thames & Hudson.

Hainge, Greg. 2013. *Noise matters: Towards an ontology of noise*. London: Bloomsbury.

Hopkins, David. 2000. *After modern art: 1945-2000*. Oxford: Oxford University Press.
Installations. n.d. *christina kubisch*.
Jarman-Ivens, Freya. 2011. *Queer voices: Technologies, vocalities, and the musical flaw*. New York: Palgrave Macmillan.
Jenkins, Henry, Ravi Purushotma, Margaret Weigel, Katie Clinton, and Alice J. Robison. 2006. *Confronting the challenges of participatory culture: Media education for the 21st century*. Cambridge, MA: MIT Press.
Kahn, Douglas. 1999. *Noise, water, meat: A history of sound in the arts*. Cambridge, MA: MIT Press.
———. 2014. Sound art, art, music. *Tacet* 3: 329–347.
Kahn, Douglas, and Gregory Whitehead. 1992. *Wireless imagination: Sound, radio, and the Avant-Garde*. Cambridge, MA: MIT Press.
Kelly, Caleb. 2017. *Gallery sound*. New York and London: Bloomsbury.
Keylin, Vadim. 2015. Unauthored music and ready-made landscapes: Aeolian sound sculpture. *Gli spazi della musica* 4: 68–85.
Kim-Cohen, Seth. 2009. *In the blink of an ear: Toward a non-cochlear sonic art*. New York and London: Continuum.
LaBelle, Brandon. 2015. *Background noise: Perspectives on sound art*. 2nd ed. New York: Bloomsbury.
Lacy, Suzanne, ed. 1995. *Mapping the terrain: New genre public art*. Seattle: Bay Press.
Licht, Alan. 2019. *Sound art revisited*. New York and London: Bloomsbury.
Lippard, Lucy R. 1997 [1973]. *Six years: The dematerialization of the art object from 1966 to 1972*. Berkeley, CA: University of California Press.
Maes, Laura, and Mark Leman. 2017. Defining sound art. In *Routledge companion to sounding art*, ed. Marcel Cobussen, Vincent Meelberg, and Barry Truax. eBook edition. Routledge.
Merleau-Ponty, Maurice. 2002 [1981]. *Phenomenology of perception*. Translated by Colin Smith and Forrest Williams. Routledge.
Motte-Haber, Helga de la. 1990. *Musik und bildende Kunst: Von der Tonmalerei zur Klangskulptur*. Laaber: Laaber-Verlag.
———, ed. 1999. *Klangkunst: Tönende Objekte und klingende Räume*. Laaber: Laaber-Verlag.
Nehls, Anselm Venezian, and Tarik Barri. 2012. #tweetscapes.
Neuhaus, Max. 1994. The Broadcast Works and Audium. In *Zeitgleich: The symposium, the seminar, the exhibition*. Vienna: Triton.
Oliveros, Pauline. 1974. *Sonic meditations*. American Music. Baltimore: Smith Publications.
———. 2005. *Deep listening: A composer's sound practice*. Lincoln, NE: iUniverse.
Russolo, Luigi. 1986 [1913]. *The art of noises*, ed. Barclay Brown. Hillsdale, NY: Pendragon Press.

Sanio, Sabine. 1999. Autonomie, Intentionalität, Situation. Aspekte eines erweiterten Kunstbegriffs. In *Klangkunst. Tönende Objekte und klingende Räume*, ed. Helga de la Motte-Haber, 67–118. Laaber: Laaber-Verlag.

Smirnov, Andrey. 2013. *Sound in Z: Experiments in sound and electronic music in early 20th-century Russia*. Cologne/New York: Koenig.

Stewart, Sharon. 2020. Inquiring into the hack: New sonic and institutional practices by Pauline Oliveros, Pussy Riot, and Goodiepal. In *The Bloomsbury handbook of sound art*, ed. Sanne Krogh Groth and Holger Schulze, 237–259. London: Bloomsbury.

Thompson, Marie. 2017. *Beyond unwanted sound: Noise, affect and aesthetic moralism*. London: Bloomsbury.

Troemel, Brad [@bradtroemel]. 2020. *Repetition mindset 3: The unwashed masses*. Instagram post.

Truax, Barry. 1984. *Acoustic communication*. Norwood, NJ: Ablex Publishing Corporation.

Ultra-red. 1996. Soundtracks.

———. 2008. *10 Preliminary theses on militant sound investigation*. New York: Printed Matter, Inc.

White, Gareth. 2013. *Audience participation in theatre: Aesthetics of the invitation*. New York: Palgrave Macmillan.

CHAPTER 3

Discourses

Abstract The main aim of this chapter is to introduce the pragmatist aesthetic of sound. It draws on the classical American pragmatism of John Dewey and G.H. Mead setting it in the dialogue with contemporary pragmatism of Bruno Latour and John Ryder. The chapter builds on Dewey's concept of art experience as a dialectic of doing and undergoing, expanding it through pragmatist approaches from a variety of disciplines from creativity studies and design theory to music sociology and video game studies, as well as suitable approaches from sound art and participatory art literature. The second half of the chapter details three principal analytical categories of the book: affordance, perspective and gesture. The term affordance refers to the opportunities for action a situation provides an agent. The notion of perspective is used by Mead to describe the way one's perceptual reality is structured by their intention to act in a certain way. In the context of participatory sound art, they offer two complimentary ways of approaching the interplay of material and social agencies: as action opportunities that artworks and social situations that arise from them provide (affordance), or as ways sound artworks (and situations) are (re)configured by action-orientations of the participants (perspective). The concept of gesture is used to discuss the participants' actions and interactions themselves and the way they unfold simultaneously in the material, social and discursive planes, particularly with a view of politics of sound art.

Keywords Sonic pragmatism • Listening and soundmaking • Sound acts • Sonic affordance • Listening perspective • Sonic gesture

3.1 Sonic, Spatial, Social

As I have shown in the previous chapter, participation is a strong thread running through much of sound art practice since its very inception. Yet as sound art and participatory art started to diverge, so did their respective discourses, leaving participatory sound art in the ever-widening theoretical gap. This chapter is an attempt to close this gap. It starts by tracing the possibilities for re-connection that persist in the theories of sound art and participatory art. From these connections I then offer a theoretical framework for participatory sound art, grounding it in pragmatist philosophy and creativity studies.

In his book *The Audible Past*, sound historian Jonathan Sterne (2003) names the moment the concept of sound was born. According to Sterne, the emergence of early sound reproduction technologies—the telephone and the phonograph—marked a shift in the cultural understanding of sound. If the pre-phonograph theories—predominantly philosophies of music and language—focused on the sources of sound—that is, musical instruments and voices, the phonograph made the ear and what it perceives the centre of attention. Where sound "had previously been conceptualized in terms of particular idealized instances like voice or music", a holistic idea of sound as an object of hearing emerged, of which "speech and music became [only] specific instances" (Sterne 2003, 2, 71).

A century later, this emphasis in conceptualisations of sound on perception over production, listening over soundmaking, remains the central focus of both the sound studies and the sound art discourse. Rooted Maurice Merleau-Ponty's (2002 [1981]) theory of perception, phenomenologies of listening (Ihde 2007; Nancy 2007; Voegelin 2010) continue to inform the philosophy and aesthetics of sound, despite the critique from post-structuralist (Kim-Cohen 2009; Kahn 2014) or new materialist (Cox 2009, 2011, 2018) camps.

This position is particularly strongly articulated in Salomé Voegelin's *Listening to Noise and Silence* (2010)—the book that came to dominate the sound art discussions in the 2010s. According to Voegelin, sound art inaugurates a particular modality of listening that entails a perceptual engagement with the world and mutual co-construction of the subject and the object. Such listening suspends the cultural and historical concerns and immerses the listener instead in the material and the sensory. Voegelin counterposes sound art listening to the kind of listening mandated by the classical music tradition: if the latter relies on the known and the foreseen, the former ventures out to explore the unknown and unforeseen.

In emphasising the agency of listening, Voegelin (2010, 38) touches on the creativity of the audience in sound art. With the visual reference bracketed away, "[t]he listener becomes producer, inventing his own contingent reality between what is heard and the time-space of its perception". At the same time, as Alan Licht (2019, 19) writes, "[s]ound art's focus on the individual is at odds with music as a connector of people and shared activity", seemingly purging sound art of its sociality. Writing a book that foregrounds the participatory and social aspects of sound art, I cannot agree with Licht here. However, this contradiction does seem to follow from listening-centred theories.

One way to resolve it comes from considering the spatial aspects of sound and sound art. Some antecedents for that can be found already in soundscape theory of the 1980s. While the mainstream acoustic ecology, following R.M. Schafer (1993), understands the soundscape simply as the spatial composition of the sonic environment, a different conceptualisation of it can be found in the works of Barry Truax. Truax (1984, xii) emphasises the socially constructed character of the soundscape, using it "not just as a synonym for 'acoustic environment', but as a basic term of acoustic communication. It refers to how the individual and society as a whole *understand* the acoustic environment through listening." A similar concept of the "aural environment" or *Klangumwelt* is put forward by Alex Arteaga (2016, 13) who contrasts it to R.M. Schafer's "realistic" understanding of the soundscape that exists independently of the actions of hearing and listening. Arteaga's (2016, 13–14) concept, on the contrary, "is developed according to the *enactive approach to cognition*" and posits that the aural environment is co-constituted by all the subjects and objects inhabiting it and emerges from "all kinds of dynamic relationships—not only the aural ones—that the listener and her environment together establish from the very moment of their encounter".

Understood thusly, aural environments can be regarded as interactive and participatory as they reflect and facilitate the functioning of the communities that inhabit them. Recent empirical studies of soundscapes show how the listeners assess soundscapes through the lens of action opportunities they afford (Nielbo et al. 2013). Truax (1984, 57) furthermore introduces the notion of "acoustic community" as a way of describing soundscapes from a social perspective—not as experiences of individual listeners but as relational formations that operate through sound. Approaching soundscapes as inherently social foregrounds the participatory aspects of soundscape compositions and soundwalks, their sonic content created by the human and non-human actors inhabiting the acoustic environment that becomes the material of the artwork.

The relational understanding of sonic spaces allows them to be both objects and tools of social critique. Gascia Ouzounian in her essay "Sound installation art: from spatial poetics to politics, aesthetics to ethics" (2013), partially adapted from her PhD dissertation (2008), approaches the spatiality of sound art from the perspective of Henri Lefebvre's theory of production of space. Lefebvre (1991) discusses how space is not merely physical space but is produced by social relations and interactions through the conceptual triad of spatial practices (creation and transformation of spaces), representations of space and representational spaces. Adopting Lefebvre's view of spatiality, Ouzounian considers how sound installations can engage not only with material spaces, but also with social and political geographies, explicating and interrogating the processes of production of space.

Similar to Ouzounian's is Brandon LaBelle's approach. By considering the spatiality of sound as a condition of its relationality, he discusses how sound reveals space to be "more than its apparent materiality" (LaBelle 2015, ix). At the same time, attending to sound's relation with space from the perspective of digital technologies and networks questions "sound's fixity, its location and specificity, as well as what and whom actually produces it" (LaBelle 2015, 256). LaBelle's more recent works *Sonic Agency* (2018) and *Acoustic Justice* (2020) undertake a project of expanding this sonic relationality beyond spatiality. Instead, he proposes rethinking acoustics as "the 'distribution of the heard' in whose practice, from rhythmical organizing to vibrational worlding, communities may work at expressions of commoning, mutuality, and what I term 'compositioning', as an improvisational, acoustic crafting in collaboration with the matters and energies of environments" (LaBelle 2020, 25). However, while he acknowledges that "sonic agency may be articulated by way of volume, and the modulation of noise and silence", his main interest nevertheless lies with "hearing and listening as what enables encounters and collaborations with otherness: as a sensing of what is often unfamiliar and unrecognizable, yet no less proximate" (LaBelle 2020, 4, 26).

Overall, thinking of acoustic space through the prism of its social function provides as useful paradigm for discussing the sociality and politics of sound. It also connects sound art theory to a well-established discourse of spatial politics and its analytical instruments. However, I am hesitant to consider participation in sound art exclusively as a function of its spatiality for two reasons. First, my contention is that space is but one mediator in the sonic interactions; putting it at the centre of discussion means diminishing the role of other mediators, which may hold equal or even higher importance to participation—such as participants' bodies or technologies. Second, my ambition in regarding participation in sound art is to approach it as a continuum, tying together individual participants' experiences with the broader social processes that they are embedded in. From this perspective, attending to participatory processes as contained within the artwork's immediate spatiality proves theoretically limiting as well.

3.2 Sense Versus Senses

Whereas sound art theories emphasise the phenomenologies of listening largely at the expense of the social, the opposite can be said of the theories of participation. The diminishing of the material can be already found in Bourriaud's (2002 [1998]) decentring of the art object. Despite many early theories of participation having the word "aesthetics" in their titles—for example, "connective aesthetics" (Gablik 1995), "relational aesthetics" (Bourriaud 2002 [1998]) or "dialogical aesthetics" (Kester 1999, 2004)—in practice, they tend to reject or at least to downplay the sensory aspects of participatory artworks in order to emphasise their sociality and politics.

For example, Grant Kester (2004, 12) writes in the introduction to his book *Conversation Pieces*:

> I give little attention to the significance of visual or sensory experience. [...] This is the level of analysis at which existing criticism is most comfortable and most effective, whereas contemporary critics and historians have found it particularly difficult to appreciate the experiences in these works that are not reducible to the visual.

Besides providing a plausible explanation for the dominance of this sociality-focused approach, this quote from Kester also reveals why sound art presents a challenge for participatory art scholarship: unlike vision, contemporary art criticism is still clearly not comfortable with sound (see, e.g., Lopez 2013).

According to Kester (2004, 2011), participatory and collaborative artworks that operate primarily through speech acts, conversations and discussions are ill-served by the traditional category of aesthetics, understood as an already-given set of norms that precede and frame the art experience for an equally already-given subject (the viewer). Instead, their dialogical aesthetics is negotiated, along with the subjectivities of the participants, in the process of the conversation on the basis of empathy. The practicing of empathy in dialogical art serves the creation of new solidarities and the enhancement of already existing ones, ultimately empowering the participants to resist the structures of oppression and transform the society.

The limitations of such an approach become evident if we consider Ultra-Red's *SILENT/LISTEN*—a bona fide conversational piece, yet to whose dialogical aesthetic and empathy-building the non-verbal sounds (and silences) are just as important as the spoken utterances. Moreover, the artists' recordings of their sessions and their later re-editing them for CDs and sound installations brings to the foreground the fact that speech acts themselves are—in their medium—sound acts (see Vannini et al. 2010). Thus, the question arises of whether dialogical aesthetics is limited to only discursive exchanges. As LaBelle (2015) notes, sound possesses the ability to transcend between bodies and arouse response in others. Participatory sound artworks engage their participants into a sonic dialogue of sorts. Despite the non-verbal character of this dialogue, arguably, the same negotiations of subjectivities and aesthetic grounds of the experience take place in such works—even though, because of this non-verbal character, they do not lend themselves well to a strictly discourse-based analysis that Kester promotes.

Claire Bishop (2012), whose heated debate with Kester has defined much of participatory art discourse in the past decades, does not give materiality much thought either. Briefly summarised, their conflict can be described as that of the ideal of collaborative art developed in horizontal interactions of the participants and pursuing social goals (Kester 2011) versus the idea of provocative forms of participation that antagonise the participants to offer them a first-person experience of social inequalities (Bishop 2012). Bishop argues for participatory art to maintain the Avantgarde's ethos of provocation and confrontation. To her this is necessary to protect the institute of authorship and, consequently, the autonomy of art—which she after Jaques Ranciere (2010) considers the fundamental source of art's political potency—from dissolving in social activism.

Bishop's thinking finds a parallel in a number of sound art critics, most famously Seth Kim-Cohen. In his book *In the Blink of an Ear*, Kim-Cohen (2009) takes to task sound art's alleged tendency to, after Cage, "let sounds be themselves" and engage in sensory delights, forgoing authorship and making the artworks politically impotent. He calls instead for explicit engagement with discursive, social and political aspects of sonic practices. Even closer to Bishop's argument, Christabel Stirling in her article "Sound art/street life" (2016) observes the negative reactions that sound artworks in the public often provoke and argues that these attest to the conflicting claims to the urban space that different groups of citizens may have. According to Stirling, in sounding out such conflicts, lies the true political potential of sound art. However, she also acknowledges that it is "not only through producing an explicit dissent and 'agonistic' struggle that sound installation art has the capacity to be political", but also through participatory practices that operate across social differences without denying them (Stirling 2016, n.p.). Interestingly, in this way, Stirling reconnects the politics of sound art to the question of its sociality.

The focus on the politics of participation and the diverging modalities of the political that it entails can thus be seen as productive, as it offers a radical shift from the solitary and somewhat solipsistic phenomenological perspective that dominates the sound art discourse. Yet including the participatory sound artworks fully within the participatory art discourse would deny them their media-specificity and the meaningful differences that stem from it. Moreover, as recent accounts show, sound may offer alternative modes of the political (see LaBelle 2018; Voegelin 2019), thus necessitating a rethinking of the politics of participation in sound art through the lens of its mediality.

3.3 Sonic Pragmatism

The fundamental differences between sound art and participatory art theories discussed above show the impossibility to merge them mechanically to attend to participatory sound art. Rather, a new theory must be built on completely new grounds that would accommodate the productive features of the two discourses while avoiding their contradictions. As I have noted in the introduction, my contention in this book is that a theory that fulfils all these conditions can be built on the basis of pragmatist philosophy, and specifically, John Dewey's aesthetics.

One particular advantage of pragmatism is that it is principally compatible with phenomenology,[1] thus allowing for a seamless integration with the existing sound art scholarship. A connection between the pragmatist aesthetics of Dewey's *Art as Experience* (1980 [1934]) and the phenomenology of sound, particularly the version laid out in Salomé Voegelin's *Listening to Noise and Silence* (2010), can already be found in both theories' emphasis on the experiential character of art. For Voegelin, the experience in question is purely perceptual, although perception is interpreted as an agentic action as opposed to passive reception. Dewey (1980 [1934], 44), on the other hand, emphasises the dialectical and interactional nature of the aesthetic experience (and experience in general), its oscillations between "doing and undergoing". While both Dewey and Voegelin agree on the bodily character of art experience, Dewey's corporealism is arguably more radical as he draws its sources from the pre-subjective interactions of the living creature with its environment. These interactions happen in cycles of the creature affecting environment and being affected by it, which emerge on every level of complexity, from most basic needs to socio-cultural processes. The experience attains an aesthetic quality when interactions reach a dynamic equilibrium—a kind of productive harmony, from which further interactions may spring.

Art for Dewey is thus, first, characterised by these cycles of doing and undergoing, and second, necessarily involves an interaction with the environment. From this follows a distinction between the art object (the product of creative process) and the artwork, defined as the experiential interaction with the art object. Moreover, Dewey insists that the cycles of doing and undergoing in interaction with the environment characterise both the artistic creation and the reception of art, resulting in principal isomorphism of expression and perception. This makes his aesthetics particularly relevant for the study of participatory art, as participation can arguably be situated in-between creation as reception.

Dewey's art theory also offers a useful change of perspective from subject-centred to relational. The prioritisation of the listening subject in sound art theory has long come under critique from both the poststructuralist and the new materialist camps. Dewey, on the other hand,

---

[1] In fact, Don Ihde's (2009) project of postphenomenology explicitly merges the two traditions.

posits a dialectical relationship between the subject and the object as they co-create each other, at least in the context of aesthetic experience. He insists on the principal relationality of art, claiming the "completeness of relations" as a necessary condition of the artistic form (Dewey 1980 [1934], 134). Such a relational perspective, once again, provides an important synthetic alternative both the phenomenology's subject-centredness and new materialism's fascination with the objects.

Importantly, this relationality necessarily presupposes a sociality: "A social relation is an affair of affections and obligations, of intercourse, of generation, influence and mutual modification. It is in this sense that 'relation' is to be understood when used to define form in art" (Dewey 1980 [1934], 134). Thus, Dewey's notion of relationality, along with his rejection of the autonomy of art and his insistence that the aesthetic experiences suffuse all spheres of life including politics and everyday, opens the door for considering the continuity of aesthetic and social forms. In this way, a pragmatist aesthetics can reconcile the phenomenological and mediality-focused perspective characteristic of sound art discourse with the questions of the politics of art that dominate the discourse of participation.

Several important concepts can be drawn from recent philosophy and art theory to expand on Dewey's aesthetics and build an analytic framework for participatory sound art. While not referring directly to Dewey, Caroline Levine (2015) offers a similar—yet even more pointed—discussion of forms. According to Levine, forms organise both matter and people, thus applying in equal measure to artistic artefacts and social formation—and crucially, easily moving between the domains of aesthetics and politics. From this perspective, it would be wrong to separate the sensory from the political (in other words, the form from the content) in participatory art the way Kester and Bishop do, as only discussing the political would limit our understanding of the artwork to only the artist's explicit intents.

This convergence of aesthetic and social forms, politics and affect, connects pragmatist aesthetics to participatory sound art. It is also characteristic of Rita Felski's (2015) project of postcritique. Examining the limits of critique as the dominant approach to the politics of art both in art practice and theory, Felski (2015, 6) points that "[c]ritical detachment ... is not an absence of mood but one manifestation of it", and as such it is riddled with its own idiosyncrasies and limitations, which affords only two positions: either the artwork performs a critique or it is complicit in the propagation of such power relations and must itself be critiqued. She argues, however, that to emphasise the affective and the sensory does not mean "to abandon politics for aesthetics", but rather to acknowledge that neither art nor politics are reducible to the intellectual detachment and scepticism of critique (Felski 2015, 18). While not rejecting critical engagement with artworks, the project of postcritique seeks a meeting point between "a willingness to suspect [and] an eagerness to listen" (Felski 2008, 22). A postcritical and pragmatist reading of sound art would thus require a double awareness: both to the affective and sensorial aspects of lived experience of sound and to the discursive and social structures that it is framed in.

Furthermore, building on Dewey's art theory, John Ryder (2020) argues in his book *Knowledge, Art and Power: An Outline of a Theory of Experience* that the political is an equally pervasive dimension of experience as the aesthetic. In other words, just as the aesthetic permeates all spheres of life, including politics, so is the political—understood as the exercise of power to effect changes in one's environment—to be found in all kinds of experience, including the aesthetic. This is not the same as to say—as is commonplace in contemporary art theory—that power relations suffuse art. Ryder posits the political as a necessary dimension of experience that is always there (meaning that it is not necessary for an artwork to explicitly engage in politics to be political) and understands power not as a hierarchical means of oppression but as agency that all actors possess (though not necessarily in equal measure).

Discussing the political experience, Ryder counterposes Chantal Mouffe's (2013) idea of democracy as driven by antagonisms and conflicts, which informs Bishop's view of participation, with Dewey's political theory, which is centred around the idea of common interests. According to Dewey (1930 [1916]), communities emerge around interests held in common by their members, and furthermore, healthy communities further pursue interests in common with other communities. While Dewey's theory is traditionally interpreted as a variation of consensual or deliberative democracy, Ryder (2020) shows that it is not necessarily so: the existence of common interests in a community does not automatically imply that all its members have all the same interests. Some of the individual's interests may lead to common pursuits with their community, while others lead to disagreements and antagonisms, making interest a more fundamental category in Ryder's view than conflict. In other words, "Deweyan view of democracy assumes the possibility and desirability not of agreement, beyond the minimum necessary for civil interaction, but of people's action toward common ends" (Ryder 2020, 182).

Thus, according to Ryder, Dewey's political theory is able to accommodate both consensual and antagonistic views of democracy. This in turn offers a possibility of reconciliation through a pragmatist aesthetics of Kester's and Bishop's approaches to participation in relation to sound art. Amplifying the agencies of the participants, participatory sound art can resonate both communality and difference—quite possibly at the same time. As, for example, Shannon Jackson (2011, 72) notes in *Social Works*, discussing both relational and community art projects that Bishop disavows, "an aesthetic intervention in civic and state processes might be its own act of estrangement or redirection, not perhaps institutional opposition but something more like infrastructural antagonism".

3.4 Sonic Doing: Acts and Gestures

Dewey's (1980 [1934]) aesthetics approaches the art experience as a dialectic of doing and undergoing. Rooting his theory in the non-interactive art of his time, Dewey describes the doing aspect as the mental reconstruction of the artist's creative process. In participatory sound art, on the other hand, the doing involves explicit acting. The participants' aesthetic experience is thus composed of the experience of their own actions, of the mediality of these actions, and of the response they provoke in the artwork and other participants. This necessitates another extension—and an update—of Dewey's aesthetics to construct an analytical apparatus for the discussion of sonic doing in the context of participatory sound artworks.

The most straightforward way to do this would be to draw on the writings of Dewey's pragmatist colleague George Herbert Mead (1938, 1972 [1934]), who formulated an extensive philosophy of acts. Two of his concepts are of particular importance for my sketch of sonic pragmatism here: perspective (understood as the way one's intention to act structures their perceptual reality) and gesture (a special kind of act aimed at provoking a response in the other)—and I will get back to them later. However, Mead did not develop an aesthetics nor art theory, which is why I have to start elsewhere.

In his book *Performing Beauty in Participatory Art and Culture*, Falk Heinrich (2014) explores the phenomenology of acts in the context of participatory art. In contrast to Kester and Bishop, he leaves out the question of the politics of participation altogether and concentrates on how one can perceive their own actions as beautiful. His understating of beauty, however, is brought up to date, as he considers it socially constructed, contextual and performative—as opposed to Kantian notion of universal disinterested pleasure.

Heinrich examines the structure of the act, which he splits into physical ("to do"), social ("to act") and discursive ("to perform") layers. His argument is that beautiful acts necessarily exhibit some sort of unity between the three aspects: "Beauty in participatory art can be described as a pleasurable experience of acts that join three dimensions—sensuous appreciations (including proprioception), agency within scripted realms, and conceptual understanding—into an experience of unity in that it affords meaning through agency" (Heinrich 2014, 178). The relations between the three layers then constitute the topology of a participatory artwork—the way participation is structured by the work's materialities.

Heinrich's model of the act is in a certain sense medium-agnostic, with the sensory dimension implicitly already including the sonic—in fact, a significant portion of his case studies comes from participatory sound art. There are three aspects to his approach, however, that are not quite satisfying in that regard. First is the medium-agnosticism itself: it is simply not his goal to consider the particular mediality of sound art. Second, although the social is a key aspect of his model, it is largely limited to one-on-one interactions between the participant and the artwork or the artist/performer. His concern is largely phenomenological emphasising the way one perceives their own actions, and not necessarily the actions of the others—even though his understanding of beauty as experience of unity can certainly be extended to social unity achieved in collective actions. This, finally, necessitates to consider the political aspect of acts. While Heinrich brackets politics out by design, this is not my intention in this book. Thus, in the following I will attempt to draw on some other sources to expand Heinrich's model fill in these gaps for my theory of sonic doing.

As I noted above, even though the mediality of sound is the central theme of sound studies, its active and pragmatic aspects rarely come into the discipline's focus. In a rare counterexample, Phillip Vannini and his co-authors in their article "Sound acts: Elocution, somatic work, and the performance of sonic alignment" (2010) contemplate what can be done with and through sound. Building on John Austin (1975) and G.H. Mead (1938), they understand sound acts as a broader version of speech acts that are not restricted to having a symbolic meaning. Like speech acts, sound acts can have locutionary (content), illocutionary (intent) or perlocutionary (effect) aspects and are performative rather than directly manipulative.

However, a special quality of sound acts, according to Vannini et al. (2010, 337), is their elocution—their ability to attract the listener's attention and provoke a rearrangement of the "sonic order"—"a sensual arrangement of sounds' material properties prevalent within a defined personal and/or social aural context". In other words, an elocutionary sound act triggers a response in kind, aimed at a "sonic alignment". Such alignment is typically understood as eradication (e.g., of noise), but can also be aimed at producing a sonic order through "positive moves that reward what is desired" (Vannini et al. 2010, 349)—such as, for example, a collective improvisation on a sound sculpture. This observation is particularly important to participatory sound art as it offers a mechanism that both mediates between individual participant's agency and the communality of participation and at the same time creates an aesthetic experience from social interaction.

A similar continuity between mediality and sociality of sound acts, but in the context of video games, is explored by Karen Collins in her book *Playing with Sound* (2013). Collins classifies sonic interactions into four categories. Physical interactions refer to the most straightforward kind of interactivity wherein physical input like pressing a button directly results in producing a sound. These are closely tied to multimodal interactions that happen between different perceptual modalities—sonic, visual, haptic etc. Interpersonal interactions occur between the players, both in the context of the game (if it is a multiplayer game) and outside of it. Finally sociocultural interactions refer to game-related sonic practices in a wider cultural context, such as performing cover-versions of in-game songs or using the game's soft- or hardware for music creation. All of those are underscored by psychological or cognitive interactions that emphasise the agentic character of perception.

In considering participation in sound art from the perspective of Collins' model, several important features come to the foreground. First, the concept of cognitive interactions recognises perceptual actions (such as listening) as a form of participation, bringing them on equal footing with expressive actions (such as soundmaking). Second, multimodal interactions reveal the mechanisms, through which the participatory processes converge with the material aspects of the work—in other words, how both the participants' actions and their sonic result constitute a single aesthetic experience. Third, socio-cultural interactions problematise the boundary between a participatory artwork and its context, as the participants' actions within the artwork exist in a continuum with their actions outside of it such as documenting or discussing their experience. Should, for example, posting online a video or audio recording of one's experience with a participatory sound installation still constitute a part of the work?

At the same time, Collins' category of socio-cultural sonic interactions does not include, at least explicitly, the political—which is a crucial aspect of participatory sound art. To address this dimension of sound acts I will thus draw on the notion of gesture, which I borrow from performance scholar Sruti Bala. In *The Gestures of Participatory Art*, Bala (2018) claims that re-acknowledging the materiality of participation is precisely what is needed to balance artistry and politics in participatory art. She proposes that participation be regarded in the gestural register—not squarely as an aesthetic phenomenon, but at the same time not only as a political act:

> Usually defined as a stance or movement of the body as a whole or a specific body part, [gesture] is simultaneously an expression of an emotional condition or an inner attitude, as well as a social habitude. It thus extends beyond the stage of theatre or performance into the sphere of public, civic life. It is a concept derived from aesthetic theory, referring to a central component of the body, language and cultural communication, and simultaneously a concept with social and political ramifications. (Bala 2018, 10)

Bala cites Giorgio Agamben's (1999, 78) notion of gesture as "the other side of language"—something that is not pre-linguistic, but anti-linguistic in a sense—that is, both opposing and intrinsically tied to signification. This understanding of the gesture is remarkably similar to how it is understood in Mead's (1938, 1972 [1934]) philosophy. As noted above, gesture to Mead is an act whose intention is to make the other act in response. From this perspective, any sound act is a gesture, as sounds are acts only "when [the others] give them meaning or affect, and when they elicit some kind of manipulative response" (Vannini et al. 2010, 332). Thus, the meaning of a sound act "resides in the response to an act, as much as it does in the material and semiotic property of the act itself" (Vannini et al. 2010, 335).

Furthermore, Bala points to the contingent character of participation, as it is composed from the gestures of the participants. She draws attention to "the unsolicited acts of participation"—the participants' actions that were not intended or even expected by the artist—as a necessary "other side" of participatory art, wherein the bulk of political meaning-making takes place (Bala 2018, 90–93). This is particularly important since most of the critiques levied at the politics of sound art or participatory art single out the artists as the sole carriers of political agency. Bala's proposal reorients the analysis of the political in art towards the participants, giving them back their agency. Such gestures carry the potential for disruption and dissent—particularly in the context of public art—but they can also be empowering or empathy-building without the artist imposing their politics of the participants.

3.5 Creative Undergoing: Agencies and Ecologies

Dewey's aesthetics has recently seen a resurgence in the creativity research. A study from 2013 led by Vlad Glaveanu (2013) tested the relevance of Dewey's framework through interviews with 60 creative professional from 5 different fields: art, design, science, scriptwriting and music, revealing various configurations of doing and undergoing in all of them. According to Glaveanu, creative processes are therefore far from being confined to the mind of a lone genius. They are necessarily interactional, with both the physical and the social worlds playing a significant role. Glaveanu (2010, 80–84) dubbed this view of creativity the "we-paradigm", as opposed to the Romantic concept of creative genius ("he-paradigm") or the dominant psychological concept of creativity as an individual trait ("I-paradigm").

Similarly influenced by Dewey, Dan Harris (2021, 17) takes this position even further, claiming that all creative agency is necessarily distributed, likening it to "a force" that "moves through but is never contained by or within. Like affects, it can instantiate or emerge, but it will never be harnessed". Suffusing "all of our natural and artificial environments", the force of creativity manifests "creative ecologies" that incorporate on equal footing both human and non-human agents (Harris 2021, 18). This convergence of humans and objects, perception and production, individual engagement and collective action is what makes the notion of creative ecology a particularly salient conceptualisation of participatory processes in sound art. Shifting focus away from the individual creator onto a multitude of people and objects, it unveils the entangled mass of creative agencies involved in the production of the sound art experience.

Two notions then become necessary to address this creative agency of the sound art's materialities: affordance and mediation. The term "affordance" was first introduced by the American psychologist James Gibson (1979), as a foundational concept for his project of ecological psychology. In Gibson's (1979, 127) original formulation, "affordances of the environment are what it offers the animal, what it provides or furnishes, either for good or ill". He stressed, however, the relational nature of affordances, situating them not fully within the environment nor within the perceiving subject (the animal). The concept of affordance was meant to overcome the dichotomy of the subject and the object, demonstrating the inadequacy of this binary opposition. The relational character of affordances has been particularly emphasised in recent literature. For example, Anthony Chemero's (2003, 189) article "Outline of a theory of affordances" redefines affordances as "relations between the abilities of organisms and features of the environment".

It is important to note that affordances are not limited to the material realm. Caroline Levine (2015) names affordances a fundamental feature of forms, explaining the flexibility and unpredictability with which they may structure reality, both aesthetic and social. Rather than imposing a predefined order, forms—much like material objects—afford possibilities to be acted upon. Moreover, their interaction in specific contexts may produce unexpected affordances or disrupt existing affordances, "results that cannot always be traced back to deliberate intentions or dominant ideologies" (Levine 2015, 8). According to Tia DeNora (2003, 48), affordance is also a mechanism of deriving meaning from abstract artforms such as music as they "serve as resources for elaborating knowledge and its categories" and "provide patterns against which that knowledge takes shape".

If the notion of affordance is useful to describe individual material agencies, their convergence is better served by the concept of mediation, particularly the way it is interpreted in actor-network theory. In his article "On Technical Mediation", Latour (1994) discusses the four possible meanings of mediation: translation, composition, blackboxing and delegation. Translation in Latour's terms refers to how interaction between different actors changes their goals and programmes of action. For example, an exhibition visitor might have a goal of aesthetic contemplation but encountering a sound sculpture may prompt them to engage in a co-creative activity. Delegation takes it one step further, changing not just the goal, but its expression as well (in the example above, the exhibition visitor starts engaging in making sounds instead of viewing the artworks). Finally, mediation can also refer to how constellations of actors assemble in a single action (composition) and how they can be perceived as a single actor (blackboxing).

The last two meanings take centre stage in Hennion's sociology of music. For Hennion (2015, 1), music "[constitutes] a whole theory of mediation in practice" as it "must always produce its object through a proliferation of intermediaries, interpreters, instruments and media". Approaching music as necessarily heterogeneous and emerging at various levels of mediation allows him to reconcile two perspectives on it: as a (monolithic) object of perception and as a (distributed) creative activity. This dichotomy of perception and production arguably becomes even more pointed in the case of participatory sound art, which makes the theory of musical mediation applicable, despite its musical and sociological roots. Participation underscores the distributed character of sound artworks, reconceptualising them as situations rather than objects (Krogh Groth and Samson 2017) and turning them into micro-societies, which prompts a social perspective. Music furthermore shares a number of soundmaking strategies with sound art, and it is by looking at mediations and mediators that the differences in these strategies can reveal themselves.

In fact, sound art has appeared in the orbit of the musical mediation theory in Georgina Born's interpretation of it. Picking up on Lydia Goehr's (1994) account of how twentieth-century experimental musical practices, including that of sound installation, undermine the modernist idea of musical work, Born (2005) uses the theory of mediation to underscore the prominent role new technologies play in reimagining the idea of musical creativity and redefining the agencies of the human and nonhuman actors involved in it. However, Born's theory does not explicitly deal with audience participation, and she prefers to pick her case studies from within the institutions and presentational formats of music.

While one of the goals of thinking creativity as an ecology is to acknowledge non-human participation in it, it is important not to forget that such ecologies include humans and their agencies as well. In principle, the notion of affordance is equally applicable to human actions—as Gibson (1979, 189) writes, "[b]ehavior affords behavior, and the whole subject matter of psychology and of the social sciences can be thought of as an elaboration of this basic fact". However, it does not explain why and how the participants decide to act or not act on specific affordances of the artwork.

For this purpose, G.H. Mead's notion of perspective becomes salient. Mead (1938, 115) defines perspective, somewhat vaguely, as "the world in its relationship to the individual and the individual in his relationship to the world", implying that the way an individual perceives the environment is contingent on the individual's acts, whether remembered or intended. In contemporary Meadian psychology, perspectives are then regarded as action-orientations—"perceptual and conceptual orientations to a situation with a view of acting within that situation" (Martin 2005, 231).

Importantly, perspectives in Mead's philosophy are not fixed but rather emergent, relational and fluid. They arise in response to a particular situation from a convergence of the actor's past experiences, their intentions to act and the affordances of the environment. Moreover, the actor is not limited to their own perspective, but can assume, with a degree of success, the perspective of another. Building upon these two traits, Glaveanu (2015, 171) describes the creative act as a dialectical process of "perspective-taking". Interacting with the affordances of their material, the actor—the artist or the participant—discovers and assumes new perspectives (including that of a prospective audience), which in turn "make previously unperceived affordances salient" (Glaveanu 2015, 168).

This notion of perspective finds a parallel in Holger Schulze's (2018) anthropology of sound and his notion of the "sonic persona". In fact, in building his concept, Schulze draws on the sound artists Bruce Odland and Sam Auinger's idea of a hearing perspective—a way one relates to the world through hearing and sound rather than through vision. The sonic persona "is shaped and constituted by the sonically perceptive, performatively generated traces, the sonic traces, that any vibrating entity leaves in a specific culture and historical era as well as in a situated sonic environment" (Schulze 2018, 123). The actions of the participants in the context of participatory sound artworks can thus be read as an aestheticised version of such "sonic traces", elevated by the frame of art. Importantly, a sonic persona, much like Meadian perspective, is not a fixed entity, but is malleable and adaptable—and thus hearing perspectives can also be communicated and taken. Moreover, Schulze extends the notion of sonic persona—and by extension, hearing perspective—to mediational entities: communities, institutions, but also apparatuses and machines.

It is worth noting that the structure of the creative acts in participatory art is more complicated than in the "traditional" process of artistic creation. First, creative acts are now performed by both the artist and the audience, which means that both sides engage in perspective-taking. Participants have to assume the perspectives of art (co-)creators, which presumably are different from their everyday perspectives of art consumers, while at the same time bringing their skills, experiences and worldviews into the frame of the artwork. Second, the "material" that the participants' creative acts transform is not raw material, but rather the "open work" in itself—something that was designed with an artistic intent and for that very purpose. Thus, creative agency in a participatory art situation emerges at the interplay between the artist's perspective—manifesting in the designed affordances of the artwork—and the perspectives of the participants, which may reveal a completely different set of affordances, unforeseen by the artist. Moreover, their relationship is further complicated by what frames the art situation: curation, its institutional or public space context, larger cultural tendencies, as well as the material agencies of the artwork's non-human mediators.

The pragmatist aesthetics of sound in its various facets discussed in the above sections forms the theoretical core of this book. As I noted in the introduction, and explicated in the first half of this chapter, participatory sound art necessitates a particular theoretical approach—connecting the material with the social, addressing creative soundmaking, and prioritising relations over subjects and objects—and a pragmatist position satisfies all these criteria. It offers analytical instruments to address both the human (perspective) and material (affordance) agencies and the ways they are exercised in acts and gestures. Moreover, drawing connections between the material, the social and the discursive sonic pragmatism offers mechanisms and models to examining the material conditions of participation, the interplay of artist and audience agencies, and the politics of participatory sound art—the subjects examined in detail in the following chapters.

References

Agamben, Giorgio. 1999. Kommerell, or on gesture. In *Potentialities: Collected essays in philosophy*, ed. Daniel Heller-Roazen, 77–85. Stanford: Stanford University Press.

Arteaga, Alex. 2016. Steps towards an architecture of embodiment: Thinking the environment aurally. In *Klangumwelt Ernst-Reuter-Platz: A project of Auditory Architecture Research Unit*, ed. Alex Arteaga, Boris Hassenstein, and Gunnar Green. Berlin: Errant Bodies Press.

Austin, John L. 1975. *How to do things with words*. 2nd ed. Cambridge, MA: Harvard University Press.

Bala, Sruti. 2018. *The gestures of participatory art*. Manchester: Manchester University Press.

Bishop, Claire. 2012. *Artificial hells: Participatory art and the politics of spectatorship*. London: Verso Books.

Born, Georgina. 2005. On musical mediation: Ontology, technology and creativity. *Twentieth-Century Music* 2: 7–36. https://doi.org/10.1017/S147857220500023X.
Bourriaud, Nicolas. 2002 [1998]. *Relational aesthetics*. Translated by Simon Pleasance and Fronza Woods. Dijon: Les Presses du réel.
Chemero, Anthony. 2003. An outline of a theory of affordances. *Ecological Psychology* 15. 181–195. https://doi.org/10.1207/S15326969ECO1502_5.
Collins, Karen. 2013. *Playing with sound: A theory of interacting with sound and music in video games*. MIT Press.
Cox, Christoph. 2009. Sound art and the sonic unconscious. *Organised Sound* 14: 19–19.
———. 2011. Beyond representation and signification: Toward a sonic materialism. *Journal of Visual Culture* 10: 145–161. https://doi.org/https://doi.org/10.1177/1470412911402880.
———. 2018. *Sonic flux: Sound, art and metaphysics*. Chicago: University of Chicago Press.
DeNora, Tia. 2003. *After Adorno: Rethinking music sociology*. Cambridge: Cambridge University Press.
Dewey, John. 1930 [1916]. *Democracy and education: An introduction to the philosophy of education*. New York: The Macmillan Company.
———. 1980 [1934]. *Art as experience*. New York: Perigee Books.
Felski, Rita. 2008. *Uses of literature*. Malden, MA/Oxford: Blackwell.
———. 2015. *The limits of critique*. Chicago: University of Chicago Press.
Gablik, Suzi. 1995. Connective aesthetics: Art after individualism. In *Mapping the terrain: New genre public art*, ed. Suzanne Lacy, 88–93. Seattle: Bay Press.
Gibson, James Jerome. 1979. *The ecological approach to visual perception*. Boston, MA: Houghton Mifflin.
Glaveanu, Vlad Petre. 2010. Paradigms in the study of creativity: Introducing the perspective of cultural psychology. *New Ideas in Psychology* 28: 79–93. Pergamon.
———. 2015. Creativity as a sociocultural act. *The Journal of Creative Behavior* 49: 165–180. John Wiley & Sons, Ltd.
Glaveanu, Vlad Petre, Todd Lubart, Nathalie Bonnardel, Marion Botella, Pierre-Marc de Biaisi, Myriam Desainte-Catherine, Asta Georgsdottir, et al. 2013. Creativity as action: Findings from five creative domains. *Frontiers in Psychology* 4. Frontiers. https://doi.org/10.3389/fpsyg.2013.00176.
Goehr, Lydia. 1994. *The imaginary museum of musical works: An essay in the philosophy of music*. Clarendon Press.
Harris, Dan. 2021. *Creative agency*. London: Springer Nature.
Heinrich, Falk. 2014. *Performing beauty in participatory art and culture*. Abingdon: Routledge.
Hennion, Antoine. 2015. *The passion for music: A sociology of mediation*. Farnham: Ashgate.

Ihde, Don. 2007. *Listening and voice: Phenomenologies of sound*. New York: SUNY Press.
———. 2009. *Postphenomenology and technoscience: The Peking University lectures*. New York: SUNY Press.
Jackson, Shannon. 2011. *Social works: Performing art, supporting publics*. Abingdon: Routledge.
Kahn, Douglas. 2014. Sound art, art, music. *Tacet* 3: 329–347.
Kester, Grant. 1999. Dialogical aesthetics: A critical framework for littoral art. *Variant*: 1–8 (supplement).
———. 2004. *Conversation pieces: Community and communication in modern art*. Berkeley, CA: University of California Press.
———. 2011. *The one and the many: Contemporary collaborative art in a global context*. Durham, NC: Duke University Press.
Kim-Cohen, Seth. 2009. *In the blink of an ear: Toward a non-cochlear sonic art*. New York and London: Continuum.
Krogh Groth, Sanne, and Kristine Samson. 2017. Sound art situations. *Organised Sound* 22: 101–111. Cambridge University Press. https://doi.org/10.1017/S1355771816000388.
LaBelle, Brandon. 2015. *Background noise: Perspectives on sound art*. 2nd ed. New York: Bloomsbury.
———. 2018. *Sonic agency: Sound and emergent forms of resistance*. Cambridge, MA: MIT Press.
———. 2020. *Acoustic Justice: Listening, Performativity, and the Work of Reorientation*. London, New York: Bloomsbury.
Latour, Bruno. 1994. On technical mediation. *Common Knowledge* 3: 29–64.
Lefebvre, Henri. 1991. *The production of space*. Oxford: Blackwell.
Levine, Caroline. 2015. *Forms: Whole, rhythm, hierarchy, network*. Princeton: Princeton University Press.
Licht, Alan. 2019. *Sound art revisited*. New York and London: Bloomsbury.
Lopez, Jay-Dea. 2013. MoMA's "Soundings" exhibition: Critiquing the critics. Blog post. *Sounds like noise*.
Martin, Jack. 2005. Perspectival selves in interaction with others: Re-reading G.H. Mead's social psychology. *Journal for the Theory of Social Behaviour* 35: 231–253.
Mead, George Herbert. 1938. *The philosophy of the act*. Chicago: University of Chicago Press.
———. 1972 [1934]. *Mind, self and society: From the standpoint of a social behaviorist*. Chicago: University of Chicago Press.
Merleau-Ponty, Maurice. 2002 [1981]. *Phenomenology of perception*. Translated by Colin Smith and Forrest Williams. Routledge.
Mouffe, Chantal. 2013. *Agonistics: Thinking the world politically*. London: Verso Books.

Nancy, Jean-Luc. 2007. *Listening*. Fordham University Press.
Nielbo, Frederik L., Daniel Steele, and Catherine Guastavino. 2013. Investigating soundscape affordances through activity appropriateness. *Proceedings of Meetings on Acoustics* 19.
Ouzounian, Gascia. 2008. *Sound art and spatial practices: Situating sound installation art since 1958*. PhD dissertation, UC San Diego.
———. 2013. Sound installation art. In *Music, sound and space*, ed. Georgina Born, 73–89. Cambridge: Cambridge University Press.
Ranciere, Jacques. 2010. *Dissensus: On politics and aesthetics*. London: Bloomsbury.
Ryder, John. 2020. *Knowledge, art, and power: An outline of a theory of experience*. Leiden and Boston: Brill-Rodopi.
Schafer, R. Murray. 1993. *The soundscape: Our sonic environment and the tuning of the world*. New York: Simon and Schuster.
Schulze, Holger. 2018. *The sonic persona: An anthropology of sound*. London: Bloomsbury.
Sterne, Jonathan. 2003. *The audible past: Cultural origins of sound reproduction*. Durham, NC: Duke University Press.
Stirling, Christabel. 2016. Sound art/street life: Tracing the social and political effects of sound installations in London. *Journal of Sonic Studies*.
Truax, Barry. 1984. *Acoustic communication*. Norwood, NJ: Ablex Publishing Corporation.
Vannini, Phillip, Dennis Waskul, Simon Gottschalk, and Carol Rambo. 2010. Sound acts: Elocution, somatic work, and the performance of sonic alignment. *Journal of Contemporary Ethnography* 39: 328–353. https://doi.org/10.1177/0891241610366259.
Voegelin, Salomé. 2010. *Listening to noise and silence: Toward a philosophy of sound art*. New York and London: Continuum.
———. 2019. *The political possibility of sound: Fragments of listening*. Bloomsbury.

CHAPTER 4

Affordances

Abstract This chapter considers participatory sound artworks from the perspective of affordance theory. Its central contention is that the material (sensory, technological, spatiotemporal) and social (participatory, relational) aspects of the artwork necessarily influence and inform each other. It uses the concept of affordance as an analytical device to investigate how participatory processes in sound art are neither limited to the artistic intent, nor completely indeterminate, being instead delimited and directed by the artwork's materialities—which they in turn reshape. The chapter first discusses three principal affordances characteristic of participatory sound artworks in general—for creativity, experimentation and connectivity. It then offers a classification of sound art's materialities and medialities into three environment types—local (not technologically extended in any way), networked, and augmented—exploring their specific affordances. Finally, the chapter expands its scope beyond the institutionally recognised forms of sound art by considering sonic practices of digital online culture that share a sound art aesthetics—both the participants' documentation of their experience with sound art on social media and the "digitally native" forms of sonic participation, such as sonic memes.

Keywords Acoustic environment • Sonic creativity • Experimental soundmaking • Sociality of sound • Augmented reality • Digital culture

4.1 Sound Artworks as Platforms

In her article "What kind of participative system? Critical vocabularies from new media art", Beryl Graham (2010) questions the traditional definition of interactive art. Since artworks are not self-aware, her argument goes, and cannot meaningfully respond to human action, merely reacting to it according to their programming, it makes more sense to call them "reactive". Instead, Graham proposes, the category of interactivity should be used to describe artworks that function as platforms through whose mediation humans can interact with each other. Consequently, she reserves the term "participation" for projects where art is fully created by the participants and merely curated by the artist.

While I have on several occasions argued that it is meaningless to distinguish between interactivity and participation in the context of sound art, irrespective of what the grounds for the distinction are (Keylin 2019, 2020), I do find the notion of the platform extremely useful to think of the relationship between the materialities of sound artworks—"the art object" in Dewey's (1980 [1934]) terms—and the aesthetic experience of participation that they facilitate. Much like the online platforms that support participatory culture, sound artworks do not dictate the exact forms that the participant interactions should take. Rather, they delineate a field of possibilities—in other words, of affordances—that the participants may or may not act upon, creating new possibilities for interaction in the process.

Thus, in this chapter, I offer an account of sound artworks from the perspective of their functioning as platforms, their affordances and the mediality of interactions that they facilitate. The following section discusses the affordances that apply more or less universally across the participatory sound art spectrum. I name three such affordances: creativity, exploration (or experimentation) and connectivity. While obviously not an exhaustive list, in my opinion, these three affordances best reflect the particular character of sound art, both underscoring the prominence of participation for the art form and distinguishing it from other participatory art practices. The third section considers affordances that stem from specific spatio-technological arrangements of sound artworks, classifying them into local, networked and augmented environment types. Finally, I consider the intersections of participatory sound art and participatory culture, pointing to a continuum between the affordances of sound artworks as platforms and creative sonic practices that emerge from online platforms themselves and their affordances.

4.2 Aesthetic Affordances[1]

4.2.1 Affordance for Creativity

The affordance for creativity refers to the audience members exercising creative agency towards the sonic aspects of the work, co-authoring it. Following the traditional music theory dichotomy of composition material and form, the participants can produce the sonic material, or arrange existing material into their own compositions, or do both.

An example of the first approach is Neuhaus' *Broadcast Works—Public Supply I–III* (1966–1973) and *Radio Net* (1977). These works were staged as live radio shows, where the participants could call the studio and perform their sounds or music. Neuhaus then mixed the content of the calls in real time and broadcasted it live, allowing the participants to improvise with him and each other. In these works, creativity is afforded at the level of individual sounds: the participants create all or most of the sonic material of the work, while the compositional structure is controlled by the artist.

Other participatory sound artworks may employ sounds pre-composed or pre-recorded by the artist, while the participants trigger and combine them, creating the compositional structure of the work. A very interesting example of this approach are Kaffe Matthews' bike operas. Since 2014, Matthews has been developing sonic bikes—bikes outfitted with loudspeakers, GPS tracking devices and sound sample banks. Riding the sonic bikes, the participants trigger various sounds, played through their bikes' loudspeakers, depending on their location, direction and speed. Here, the participants have no control over the sonic material; however, the affordance for creativity is expressed in how their actions and interactions shape the form of the composition produced from these predefined sounds.

The two approaches can be combined too. The Baschet brothers' sound sculptures allow the participants to play any sounds they can get out of the sculpture in any sequence or combination they want. While the

---

[1] The material of this section has previously appeared in Keylin, Vadim. 2020. Crash, boom, bang: Affordances for participation in sound art. *SoundEffects* 9: 98–11. The text was edited for the purposes of this book.

acoustic qualities of the sculptures are designed by the artists, their soundmaking affordances, being relative to the participants interacting with the sculpture, are never limited to what the artists intended. Similarly, participatory sound installations may employ their spatial structures as open-ended scores for the participants' soundmaking. In Kathy Hinde's *Vocal Migrations* (2012), the participants are blindfolded and asked to navigate a paper labyrinth through echolocation: they record vocal calls into a hand-held device, which then transforms their voices based on proximity of the walls and other participants and plays them back. The processed voices of the participants merge together into an improvised electroacoustic choir piece that arises from the installations spatiality in a non-linear fashion.

Finally, as discussed in the previous chapter, listening itself can be a creative activity. This is especially true in the context of sound installations, where the listeners arrange the spatially distributed sounds into a durational work that is unique to them through their listening. At the same time, this sort of listening has a performative aspect as well. For example, soundwalking engages participants in an activity that breaks with the order of the everyday, casting them as performers in a Happening or a Situationist *derivé*. Furthermore, the participants produce a variety of intentional and unintentional "sonic traces" (Schulze 2018, 111) in the process, which become part of both the listening experience and the physical performance.

The affordance for creativity in a general sense is something shared by most participatory art practices irrespective of their media. However, the character of the sonic medium exerts a significant influence on how this creativity is realised evident in the two further affordances—for exploration and for connectivity.

4.2.2 Affordance for Exploration and Experimentation

In the previous subsection, I described the affordance for creativity in general musical terms as this is currently the only language we have to address sound-related creativity. However, the soundmaking activities that the affordance for creativity facilitates are distinctly different from the musical affordances. First and foremost, they are characterised by a lack of musical *intent*. Particularly in works that rely on spatial distribution of sounds, the temporal compositional structure is a by-product of the participants' actions rather than their end goal. The way they interact with the artwork is primarily exploratory and experimental, leading the way for the second participatory affordance I want to discuss here.

The affordance for exploration refers to several aspects of participatory sound artworks. First, the participants in such works are not necessarily trained musicians, and even if they are, they are not familiar with how a particular work operates (at least not the first time they encounter it). Their initial engagement with the work is driven by curiosity, the desire to uncover the sonic potential of the work and how this potential relates to the immediately visible elements. The cycles of doing and undergoing are most evident here as the participants try out different actions to hear what sounds they produce and plan their next actions based on what they hear. Some of Kaffe Matthews' sonic bike rides have the word "games" in their titles (*The Pedalling Games*, 2014; *The Coventry Pedalling Games*, 2015 etc.), emphasising the playful and experimental nature of this kind of sonic engagement. The artist challenges the "players" to figure out what actions are required to activate this or that sound, both from their own experience with the work and from watching others play. In many ways, it is a process similar to the gameplay loop of augmented reality games, such as *Pokémon Go*.

Furthermore, the participants in sound artworks are not even expected to produce a musical result that would comply to set aesthetic criteria or even be identified as musical or artistic. Some of the Baschet sculptures were designed specifically with non-musicians or people with disabilities in mind, replacing the traditional musical scales and harmonic relations with a palette of timbres (Baschet and Baschet 1987). These sculptures resemble traditional instruments just enough to suggest that they should be played but are alien enough so as not to create specific expectations of what could or should be done with them.

Another aspect of the affordance for exploration is the lack of specific instructions—scripts or scores—telling the participants what exactly they have to do. While the spatial structure of a sound installation can function as a score, as noted in the previous subsection, these are necessarily open-ended and indeterminant. Even in guided soundwalks, arguably the most directed form of participatory sound art, there is enough leeway for the participants not to follow the guide, directing their listening to the sounds that catch their attention or spontaneously engaging in soundmaking with the objects in environment.

Finally, the connection between the participants' actions and their sonic result is often unobvious, or even obscured. For example, the online installation *#tweetscapes* (2012) by Anselm Nehls and Tarik Barri discussed in

Chap. 2 used a complex algorithm to translate Twitter posts into sounds. While an individual tweet would have an immediate effect on the work's sound, the obscured principles of the text-to-sound transformation and the high number of events happening simultaneously at any given time made it impossible to predict—or sometimes even discern—exactly what that effect would be. The affordances of *#tweetscapes* thus enforce experimentation by hindering the more traditionally musical modes of soundmaking.

4.2.3 Affordance for Connectivity

In the introduction to his book *Background Noise: Perspectives on Sound Art*, Brandon LaBelle (2015) claims that sound is an inherently relational phenomenon. The affordance perspective, with its focus on relations and interactions between actors, supports such a reading of sound. As discussed in the previous chapter, sound in participatory sound art exists in a dialectical unity of doing and undergoing, being the object of both aesthetic production and reception, often at the same time. Moreover, it is inextricably linked, on the one end, to the material and medial components of the artwork and, on the other end, to the listener-participant, establishing a relation between the two.

Similarly, it can be said that sound in sound art serves to establish interpersonal relations between the participants as well. LaBelle (2015, xi) describes this phenomenon in connection with the spatial properties of sound, stating that "sound as relational phenomena [*sic*] immediately operates through modes of spatiality". He proceeds to name three consequences of this spatiality: that "sound is always in more than one place", that it "occurs among bodies" and, finally, that "sound is never a private affair", always carrying with it a social dynamic (LaBelle 2015, xi–xiii). The order of these consequences is important, as it indicates causality: sound is spatial; therefore, it connects the objects (bodies) in space, and thus facilitates relations between them. In other words, for LaBelle the sociality that sound art produces is a consequence of its spatiality.

The connection between spatiality and relationality of sound is hard to deny; however, I would argue that it is better stated in terms of affordance than causality. Space does not cause the sonic connection between the bodies but affords it. Similarly, this connection does not necessarily lead to a tangible sociality but affords and encourages it. It is not a necessary condition either: as I will show in the next section, participatory sound artworks may operate through bypassing physical space to establish connections over large distances and other barriers.

I call this ability of sound to establish relations the affordance for connectivity. Arguably, it finds its most prominent expression in the form of collaborative performances facilitated by sound artworks. Giving the participants the means to produce sound and placing them in a shared environment, physical or virtual, invites a non-verbal sonic dialog between them. This affordance is particularly prominent in virtual environments, like that of Neuhaus' *Broadcast Works*. The materiality of such works is confined to a virtual space and not immediately accessible to the participants; instead, it serves as a means for them to enter a collaborative soundmaking process. However, collaborative aspects may be equally prominent in physical environments as the case of the Baschets' sculptures shows. In an exhibition situation, sound sculptures and their players inhabit a shared acoustic space where listening to other participants' soundmaking invites one to enter into a sonic dialog with them.

At the same time, sound's ability to establish relations leads to the distinction between the participants and the secondary audience (i.e., the audience not involved in co-creative processes) largely dissolving. A rider on Matthews' sonic bike broadcasts their sounds onto the public space, attracting attention and prompting interactions with the passers-by, who, initially, might not even be aware of a sound artwork taking place. Even a silent group of soundwalkers disturbs the ordinary order of the everyday and prompts social encounters just as well as sonic bike riders do—precisely because of the walkers' silence (Polli 2017).

Finally, the affordance for connectivity can also happen across the human-non-human divide. In her recent article "On nonhuman sound: Sound as relation", Georgina Born (2019) calls for abandoning the subjective and anthropocentric models of sound, reconceiving it instead as a relational and mediational phenomenon that transcends the subject-object dichotomy. The "acoustic community" (Truax 1984, 57) that the participants in a soundwalk connect to—and fleetingly become part of—through their listening is composed by both humans and non-human agents that shape the sonic environment they inhabit.

4.3 Technological Environments[2]

Both sound art and music largely rely on the same networks of mediators: sound sources (instruments, voices), soundmakers (human or non-human), spaces of soundmaking and their acoustic parameters, recording and transmission technologies etc. One major difference, however, is in how sound art purposefully brings its mediators to the foreground, making them part of the aesthetic experience. The shapes of the Baschet sculptures, the physicality of riding a sonic bike, the spatial organisation of Neuhaus' installations—all these elements are simultaneously aesthetic agents and devices for listening and soundmaking. Even the sounds they produce, reproduce or transform have a dual role, being the aesthetic product of the participants' interactions as well as one of the mediators, through which the participants—both human and non-human—can relate to each other.

In other words, the materiality of a sound artwork is defined not only by sound, but in equal measure by all sorts of nominally silent—visual, spatial, technological—actors that act upon sound and transform it. However, by transforming sound, these actors transform the relational structures that sound facilitates and mediates—and thus the affordances that support them. In the following, I suggest a classification of sound art environments based on the extent and type of their technological extensions. These three types are local (not technologically extended in any way), networked (connecting discreet spaces through media channels) and augmented (overlaying physical and virtual environments onto each other). In all three cases my focus lies with how the medialities of these technologies structure the participants' interactions.

4.3.1 Local Environments

Of the three environment types named above, local is the hardest to define, but I also have to start with it, as it is the "default" type against which other, more specific kinds of environments (networked, augmented) take shape. I am using the term "local" to stress that these environments

---

[2] The material of this section has previously appeared in: Keylin, Vadim. 2019. Medialities of participation in sound art. In *Cultures of participation: arts, digital media and cultural institutions*, ed. Birgit Eriksson, Carsten Stage, and Bjarki Valtýsson, 129–146. New York: Routledge. Reproduced with permission of Informa UK Ltd. through PLSclear. The text was edited for the purposes of this book.

are not intentionally technologically extended in any way. In other words, local environments refer to definite continuous spaces that do not have other, physical or virtual, spaces connected to them through telematics communication channels—or if they do, such connections are not presented as part of the artwork and the aesthetic experience. The space in question can be of any scale—a gallery room or a whole city—however, the participants must have the ability to traverse the whole of it physically.

Sound artworks that do not have any sort of digital components and rely only on mechanical means of interactivity—such as the Baschets' sound sculptures—are the most obvious case of a local environment. However, such environments are not exclusive of digital elements altogether. Various sensors, sound-generating and controlling technologies can be part of local environments as well. For example, Liz Phillips' interactive sound installations such as *Sound Structures* (1971), *Responsive Spaces* (1974) or *City Flow* (1977) used electronic sensors to respond to the participants' movements with distinctly synthesised sounds. However, these works contained the sound control, sound generation and playback in the same physical space, and thus should be classified as local environments. Therefore, the important conditions for defining local sound art environments are that listening, soundmaking and interacting with each other should be conducted in the same physical space and that listening should not require personalised mobile devices.

Sound artworks in local environments can be situated between two "poles" exemplified by the practices of sound sculpture and soundwalk. While sound sculptures focus on separate physical sound sources, which could be situated in any space, soundwalks instead explore specific acoustic spaces, whose sonic content at the moment of performance is largely uncontrolled by either the artist or the participants. However, most sound artworks in local environments take the form of sound installations, which can be regarded as a middle ground between the two practices, as they emphasise the interplay between the sound sources and their spatial distribution.

Local environments possess two principal qualities that are reflected in the affordances of sound artworks situated therein, even when they are as diverse as sound sculptures and soundwalks: continuity and immediacy. Continuity means that the spaces where such works happen are not segmented into discrete sites (as happens with networked environments) or overlaying planes (augmented environments), which makes these spaces freely traversable for both sound and the participants. As the example of the Baschets' sculptures shows, the locality of the exhibition affords a musical dialog between the audience members. A sound produced by one participant fills the room and necessarily reaches the ears of another, prompting a response. At the other end of the spectrum, in artworks that rely on creative listening rather than soundmaking, continuity allows the participants to traverse the space and reconfigure their spatial relations with the sound sources. In other words, simply walking through the space, the participants of soundwalks create personal compositions from sounds supplied by their surroundings.

This affordance of continuity reflects Max Neuhaus' intention behind the sound installation—to place the sounds in space instead of time for the listener to recompose them. For him, this was the difference between sound installation and music; however, the same operation can be applied to music as well. A classic example of this is Janet Cardiff's *The Forty Part Motet* (2001), whose sound material is a composition by Renaissance composer Thomas Tallis. Cardiff dismantled the motet into separate parts, each assigned to a single loudspeaker, so that the listeners could move inside the piece, experiencing harmonic relations as structures of space. By spatially distributing a musical piece, she imbued the listeners with an agency to compose their personal reading of it, which they are normally denied in a musical context.

While space can transform sound, sound, traversing and filling the continuous spaces of local environments, can also transform them in turn. For example, *Traffic Mantra* (1991) by the artist duo O+A (Bruce Odland and Sam Auinger) was a sound installation at the Trajan's Forum in Rome. The artists used ancient Roman amphorae, found on site, to filter the extraordinarily noisy soundscape of the Forum and played the results back onto the site. Their approach can be described as "sonic recycling": the installation gathers the acoustic "trash" of accidental participants and turns it into harmonious tones, making the ambiance of the space more inviting. The reinvention of public space, in turn, encourages social encounters between passers-by (Föllmer 1999).

The second aspect, immediacy, refers to the fact that in local environments, the participants, sound sources and sounds are all physically present in the same space. Consequently, the affordances of sound artworks in local environments have a stark corporeality to them. Such artworks do not have depersonalised interfaces, but rather translate the physical gestures and movements into sonic experiences. This immediacy is most evident when the participants' bodies are themselves sound sources, like in *Vocal Migrations* discussed in the previous section.

Nevertheless, the corporeal connection holds even when the gesture in question is minimal, like in Harry Bertoia's sound sculptures. These sculptures made of multiple colliding metallic rods require only that the listener sets them into motion initially. However, this initial gesture exerts a direct influence on the character of the rods' movement, while the tactile experience of touching them makes evident the materiality of sound. Similarly, in the sensor-based works such as those of Phillips or Peter Vogel, the sound's speed and direction correspond to the speed and direction of the listener. At the same time, the relationship between movement and sound is reciprocal: as the participants' actions effect sonic result, the sounds produced also influence further movements. For example, Vogel's sound sculpture *Berlin Sound Wall* played techno music for the listeners to dance to; in turn, their dance moves, registered by light sensors, defined what music was played.

The corporeal and immediate character of sound art in local environments helps dispel the aura of elitism associated with "high art". Playing a sound sculpture or an interactive sound installation does not imply an expectation of virtuosity, while listening to environmental sounds finds aesthetic value in the mundane. On the other hand, the corporeal character of such works, their insistence on primarily physical interactions, may also become exclusory, for example, for participants with physical disabilities.

4.3.2 Networked Environments

Networked environments, which could be also called distributed or telematic, are characterised by the flow of information between several physical locations connected through technological channels. The most obvious example of that is the internet. In Chap. 2, I have already discussed two kinds of networked sound artworks: the "shared sonic environments" (Barbosa 2003, 57), such as *Auracle*, and social data mining and sonification projects like *#tweetscapes*.

However, networked environments are not limited to the internet. The flow of sonic information can be organised through analogue means like radio or telephone as well. For example, Neuhaus described *Auracle* as the next step in his *Broadcast Works, highlighting the continuity between the digital and the analogue networks*. At the same time, new mobile technologies bring with them new networking protocols, like Wi-Fi or Bluetooth.

Finally, the same work may combine both analogue and digital channels. For example, Benoît Maubrey's series *Speaker Sculptures* (1987–present) are large-scale sound sculptures in public spaces built of loudspeakers and often modelled after existing buildings or building types. Most of these works are connected both to the phone lines and the internet (or other types of digital networks), allowing the participants to speak or play music through the sculptures. This further shows how networked sound art environments can connect the public space, where the sculpture is installed, to a multitude of private spaces, where the participants are located.

Analysing the networked environments and their affordances as a whole, both a certain continuity emerges, and some functional differences between the digital and analogue ones. The similarities stem from the fundamental principle of connectivity. Sound artworks in networked environments can also be categorised, following Franziska Schroeder and Pedero Rebelo (2017), as "distributed sounding art". According to Schroeder and Rebelo (2017, 439–440), three aspects form the core of distribution: assignment ("parts or fragments of an entity are allocated to groups or individuals according to a particular process or intention"), transport ("dislocation of an entity [...] across two or more locations") and sharing ("a distribution of resources [...] while certainly implicating human agency and notions of reciprocity"). These three aspects and their respective affordances characterise the whole continuum of distributed sound artworks irrespective of the technological means of distribution.

Network expands the space and time of sound artworks, allowing them to accommodate for larger amounts of participants than any given physical space would. Such works do not necessarily require the participants to be physically present, which potentially affords participation to people that would not be able to engage with the work otherwise. At the simplest level, the network allows to overcome distance. It can also afford access to performing in public space from the safety of the private one, like in *Speaker Sculptures*, or like in *Auracle*, providing the opportunity for collective music-making to people too socially anxious to try this in a physical setting. However, the network may also create barriers, as its accessibility relies on technologies that may be themselves inaccessible to people who cannot afford them or lack technological literacy.

While both digital and analogue networks connect spaces, the nature of information flows is vastly different between the two. Digital networks can transmit any type of information, which may then be transformed into sound, while analogue audio channels typically only transmit sound.

Therefore, the participants' voices constitute the majority of sonic material in analogue networked sound art, particularly when phone lines are used. The exceptions here are the works that transmit sounds from public spaces, like Maryanne Amacher's *City Links: Buffalo* (1967). In this work, the sounds from five microphones installed in the streets of Buffalo were broadcast in real time by the local radio station for 28 hours. While the majority of the sounds that composed the work were not vocal in nature, they were still produced by the unwitting participants in the context of their immediate surroundings, not with the means of the work. Digital networked environments, on the other hand, typically present the participants with some sort of graphical UI for their soundmaking. For example, in Chris Brown's *Eternal Network Music* (2003) the characteristics of the synthesised voices were determined by the user moving their mouse. *Auracle* is a rather peculiar case in that regard as its input method relies on the user's voice; however, it is not transmitted, but rather analysed and broken down into control information for sound synthesis. Other input options include sharing the user's sound files, like in later *Speaker Sculptures* such as *The Obelisk* (2019), or relying on the data provided by social media, like in *#tweetscapes*.

Network mediation, whether it manifests as synthesis algorithms, sound filters or merely latency and mixing, means that the soundmaking process in networked sound art lacks the immediate corporeality of works in local environment. The connection between the participants' actions and their sonic result is often unobvious, or even obscured by mixing techniques (*Broadcast works*) or complex synthesis algorithms (*Auracle*, *#tweetscapes*). This connection is even more unobvious to other participants, who can only hear the sounds produced, but cannot observe soundmaking actions.

Moreover, while the network connects spaces, it also separates actors, as listening and soundmaking in such works often happen in different spaces. The spaces in question can be different physical sites, like the private and public spaces of *Speaker Sculptures*, or different websites, like in *#tweetscapes*, which uses Twitter for input and its own site for output. In turn, this separates participants and listeners into two functionally different, if potentially overlapping, groups. In *Speaker Sculptures*, for example, the off-site callers cannot hear the sonic output of the sculpture, while the on-site listeners may not have a phone on them to call it. Similarly, in *#tweetscapes*, only German Twitter users provide data for sonification, which anyone could listen to, but these participants may not be even aware of the existence of the work and their role in it.

At the same time, the dislocation of actors and processes across different spaces provides an affordance of its own—an affordance for asynchronicity. That is to say, participation in such environments does not have to happen at the same time and space as its sonic result. In its simplest form, it can be realised as an asymmetric connection like that of *Speaker Sculptures*, where the sounds are transmitted from private spaces to the public, but not the other way, providing a more controlled and comfortable environment for the callers who otherwise might become overwhelmed by the rich soundscape of the sculpture and its urban context. Other works implement temporal asynchronicity. For example, in Jason Freeman's *Piano Etudes* (2005) the participants do not provide sounds but contribute to a modular score for live performance. Atau Tanaka's *Prométhée Numérique/Frankenstein Netz* (2003) was an online installation presenting a "living data-organism" composed of text, sound and image files "fed" to it by the participants, to which it replied in SMS messages demanding more (Tanaka 2018, n.p.). The material collected this way was then used in a live electroacoustic performance. Such works allow the participants to choose not only the site of their participation, but time as well.

4.3.3 Augmented Environments

The term "augmented reality" is generally defined as "a real-time direct or indirect view of a physical real-world environment that has been enhanced/*augmented* by adding virtual computer-generated information to it" (Carmigniani and Furht 2011, 3). While the original idea of augmented reality referred specifically to the introduction of virtual images into one's normal vision field (Caudell and Mizell 1992, 660), later literature expanded the concept, applying it to all human senses, including hearing. The "virtual" in augmented reality is also not necessarily equated with "computer-generated" but can generally refer to information not normally available to human senses without technological means (Carmigniani and Furht 2011, 3–4). Finally, sensory information may be removed rather than added as well—a technique some researchers dubbed "diminished reality" (Azuma et al. 2001, 34).

Therefore, in this chapter, I am using the term "augmented (acoustic) environment" to refer to an environment that overlays a virtual acoustic space (accessed through some kind of technology) onto a physical one, either merging with or overwriting the original soundscape. As noted above, the virtual elements of the augmented acoustic environments do not have to be computer-generated, and the technology used to access it does not have to be digital. In fact, Max Neuhaus' original sound installation *Drive-In Music* (1968) can be considered an example of an augmented environment, as its sounds have to be accessed through the listener's car radio. A more pronounced example is Christina Kubisch's *Electrical Walks* (2003–present)—a series of soundwalks employing wireless headphones that implement the principle of electromagnetic induction to translate the electromagnetic disturbances in the environment into sound. The sources of such disturbances can be manifold: from ATMs and anti-theft gates to power cables and cars. Designing an *Electrical Walk* in a given city, Kubisch first scouts the city herself, noting musically interesting spots. The audience members are then given a set of inductive headphones, a suggested route, containing the previously discovered listening points, and let to explore freely. Though substituting the original soundscape with electromagnetic one would technically classify the acoustic environment of *Electrical Walks* as "diminished", the experience of the artwork is not only a listening experience; it is necessarily multimodal. Thus, as a whole, the participants' reality can still be thought of as augmented as their visual and haptic perception of space is extended through the virtual sonic plane.

While not necessarily digital, the technologies used in augmented sound art environments do have to be mobile and personalised, as simply broadcasting the sounds into the environment would make them part of the soundscape and would not create a separate acoustic plane. That is not to say that such works necessarily have to be headphones-based. While sounds played by Kaffe Matthews' sonic bikes are broadcast into the environment, I still classify her works as belonging to augmented environments for two reasons. First, each sonic bike's loudspeakers have limited sound volumes, thus creating a local acoustic space around them that exists on a much smaller scale than the space of the work as a whole. Second, the sounds played by an individual bike depend entirely on its position, direction and the cyclist's speed and are not affected by the actions of other participants. This makes the acoustic environment of an individual participant highly personalised despite the public character of the sonic playback.

The affordances of augmented sound art can be situated along two primary axes. The first axis concerns where the sounds are coming from— whether they are placed in the environment by the artist, or they already exist there, but are not accessible without the use of technology. In the latter case, the sounds may be real-time sonifications of other features of the environment, as in *Electrical Walks*, or come from a variety of special microphones used to access normally inaudible sounds. For example, in Iain Armstrong and Annie Mahtani's soundwalk in Ponta Delgada during the *Invisible Places* conference in 2017 both hydrophones and contact microphones were used to augment the listening experience. Such practices afford the participants an extended perception of the environment, stirring curiosity and encouraging exploration.

On the other hand, practices that place sounds into the environment extend the environment itself. While sonic bikes are a technology specific to Kaffe Matthews' practice, many artists use smartphones' GPS tracking capabilities to achieve similar effect. For example, Teri Rueb's soundwalks take the form of smartphone apps that overlay the space with narrated stories, musical sounds and field recordings to achieve a condensed sense of place. Another interesting example is Mark Shepard's *Tactical Soundgarden Toolkit* (2006), which turns this principle upside down, allowing the participants to introduce the sounds into the virtual environment. Shepard's project invokes the practice of guerrilla gardening, inviting the users to "plant" sounds in various locations, hear sounds planted by other users and, if they wish so, "prune" them, changing the sound's parameters.

Augmented reality artworks with artist-authored sound material afford the same kind of creative listening as sound installations and soundwalks. However, keeping the sounds hidden in the virtual plane, waiting to be activated by the participants, instead of openly broadcasting them emphasises the listeners' agency and makes the whole process of re-composing more tangible. At the same time, it also affords unpredictability and experimentation, as the character of the sounds cannot be discerned from their location beforehand.

The other axis is the way sounds are accessed: through headphones or loudspeakers. Headphones constrain the virtual components of the work to the listener's private space, leading to a more personalised experience. Outside the realm of sound art, this is exemplified by the phenomenon of silent discos—dance parties that are largely silent to an outsider as the participants dance to the music played only through their headphones. The headphones also cut off the natural soundscape, substituting it fully with the virtual one, which affords greater immersion and stronger perspective change. On the other hand, the advantage of loudspeakers is that broadcasting sounds into the environment encourages interpersonal interactions, both with other participants and the passers-by. The experience of such works is therefore more social, even though such interactions are not always necessarily friendly as publicly broadcast sounds might provoke antagonistic reactions.

Space plays a primary role in the affordance structure of mobile sound art. The sonic overlay over the existing urban space makes the participants' interactions necessarily multimodal, as every action occurs at both the physical and the virtual planes. Typically, as noted in the previous section, space serves as a sort of open-ended score for the participants' listening or soundmaking. This relationship can be subverted, however, as is the case in Janet Cardiff's soundwalks, for example *The Missing Voice (Case Study B)* (1999). In this work, it is the sonic material that directs the participants' engagement with and movement though space, creating a dissociation between the two perception channels.

Augmenting either the participants' perception of space or the space itself, mobile sound art encourages reassessment of the role and character of the space (particularly urban and public space). Ksenia Fedorova (2016, 46–47) links sound art using locative media to the discipline of critical cartography, which seeks to "engage political and social underpinnings" behind spatial structures. At the same time, this reliance on space carries an exclusory potential. To become a participant in mobile sound artworks, one has to have access to the public space, which may be denied to them, e.g., by disability. The opportunities for participation may be further limited by requiring a certain skill (e.g., biking), or certain income level (e.g., works for smartphones).

4.4 Beyond the Artwork

While the classification discussed above addresses the range of participatory technologies employed in sound artworks, the increasingly technologised and connected landscape of today's culture makes it hard, if not impossible, to determine the boundaries of the artwork and the art experience and consequently between the different environment types. For example, most potential participants in sound artworks possess smartphones that they can use to make photos of the artwork, record the sounds they make or even livestream their experiences privately or publicly. Should such actions be considered belonging to the immediate experience of the artwork or to its afterlife? On the one hand, they do not directly respond to the artwork's materiality or structure and its affordances. On the other hand, they are nevertheless facilitated by the artwork and tethered to the participants' aesthetic experience. Although such questions and considerations accompany more or less all art in the digital age, solving them becomes particularly complicated in case of participatory art due to its necessarily contingent character, whereby the audience's experience is already shaped by their actions.

This issue is thrown into particularly sharp relief in case of networked environments. For example, any discussion of *#tweetscapes* happening in the German segment of Twitter would be fed back into the work's sonification engine. Similarly, Maubrey's speaker sculpture *Speakers' Arena* (discussed in detail in the next chapter) sonified Twitter posts marked with the #speakersarena hashtag. However, as the hashtag simply restates the name of the artwork, many participants used it for posts documenting their experience. In that way, both discussions (in case of *#tweetscapes*) and documentations (in case of *Speakers' Arena*) of the artworks became a form of interacting with them, a kind of "metaparticipation".

Through the use of mobile technologies, the participants may extend the borders of the artwork not only conceptually, but also spatially, as was again the case of *Speakers' Arena*. As documented by their Twitter exchange, a participant in Berlin initiated a happening of sorts with some of his friends from other cities, who were interested in the sculpture, but could not travel to Berlin to experience it first-hand. He thus invited them to post on Twitter with the #speakersarena hashtag during a specified time frame. He would then creatively videotape the *Arena* sonifying the tweets—choosing interesting angles and applying video filters—and post the videos back as a reply to the originators. The mobile technologies and the participant's actions thus served as a means for others to become participants and experience the artwork. However, the experience they received was not the immediate experience of the artwork but mediated by the creative agency of the person who initiated the happening and made the videos.

In Collins' (2013) model of sonic interactions in video games discussed in the previous chapter, she distinguishes between the interactions happening within the game and outside of it. However, she notes that some interactions—for example, interpersonal ones—can happen on either side of the medium's boundary, and even across it. In her model, the examples above can be classified as socio-cultural interactions—happening on a larger spatiotemporal scale than the medium itself, yet still tethered to it and shaped by the materialities and affordances of the medium.

At the same time, considering the participants' actions happening outside the artwork, yet connected to it, as part of the sound art experience establishes a continuum between participatory sound art and creative sonic practices in participatory culture. These practices are not facilitated or inspired by institutionally acknowledged sound artworks but rather by everyday objects and technologies whose sonic affordances the participants in online communities find interesting to engage with. Two of the most prominent such objects and technologies are rubber chickens and autotune software.

Rubber chickens have been used as comedy props since at least early 1900s. These rubber toys are made in shape of chickens—or, sometimes, other birds like ducks—and equipped with a reed that makes a sound when the toy is pressed. Notably, the sonic mechanism of the toys is pneumatic rather than electronic and similar in structure to animal or human vocal tract, meaning that by manipulating the toy's "body" the pitch and timbre of its "voice" can be varied.

Because of the striking contrast between their silly appearance and their robust sonic affordances, the rubber chickens have taken the internet by storm since the late 2000s. The early viral videos—that can be described as "sonic memes"—were inspired in particular by the fact that, when pressed in a certain way, the toys make a sound that uncannily resembles a human scream. Later videos saw rubber chicken find a variety of uses, from playing classical tunes to much more experimental and projects. Some of the "sound sculptures" created by internet users by attaching several rubber chickens together and/or placing them on water faucets or car exhaust pipes show inventiveness and creativity, both conceptual and sonic, that can rival much of institutionally acknowledged sound art.

Another widespread genre of sonic experimentation online concerns the use of autotune software. Offered by several companies, these vocal filters are meant to correct the pitch of the singers when recording in studios, but on particularly aggressive settings produce a characteristic robotic sound. This effect is also occasionally purposefully used by musicians. However, the internet users have quickly figured out that the input material does not have to be sung and the context does not have to be musical. Autotune has been applied in viral videos to a variety of sound sources—from news clips to screaming cats and other animals.

While the practice itself derives its aesthetic—mostly comedic—effect from simply defamiliarising the human and non-human voices, in some cases it has developed into more artistically elaborate genres. For example, "autotune stories" on TikTok are videos of the users recounting their deeply personal or embarrassing (or both) experiences—such as coming out or going on a bad date—in autotuned voices. These videos can be described as a kind of sound poetry or digital oral poetry, as they exhibit the traits of both traditional oral literature (storytelling focus, musicalisation) and literary lyric poetry (subjective expression), while at the same time being facilitated by the digital technology and culture.

In *Art as Experience*, Dewey (1980 [1934], 5) writes insightfully: "[s]o extensive and subtly pervasive are the ideas that set Art upon a remote pedestal, that many a person would be repelled rather than pleased if told that he enjoyed his casual recreations, in part at least, because of their esthetic quality". Similarly, the creators of the videos described above would likely be opposed to the idea that what they are making is sound art. However, the cultural context in which these practices emerge and the sounding objects and audio technologies that inspire them share the same basic affordances—for creativity, experimentation and connectivity—as the institutionally acknowledged works of participatory sound art discussed above.

4.5 Materiality and Sociality

Considering sound artworks as interactive or participatory platforms defined by their affordances forms the first step towards a pragmatist aesthetics of sound art in its material-social unity, building on Dewey's (1980 [1934]) original idea of thinking aesthetic experience as operating in cycles of doing and undergoing. While the sonic *doing*—the creative acts of participants—lies at the core of participatory sound art experience, it occurs in a constant dialog with material components of the artwork, whose agencies the participants *undergo*. The concept of affordance offers a way to describe these complex relations between the various actors involved in a participatory sound artwork, exposing the mechanisms through which these relations negotiated.

In this chapter, I have identified three high-level aesthetic affordances that sound artworks possess: for creativity, for experimentation, and for connectivity, though this list is by no means exhaustive. While participatory sound art shares some of these affordances with participatory art in general, sound plays a pivotal role in how they function in sound art and determines the specific character of participation. First, sound is processual and happens in real time, which allows for spontaneous, emergent and non-directed forms of creative or political activities. It facilitates a particular form of co-authorship, where the artist creates the conditions for the participants to exercise their creative agency but does not influence their actions beyond that. Second, sound invites listening and replying, instigating a non-verbal sonic dialog between the participants and encouraging their collaboration with each other, once again, without being instructed to do so. The dialogical nature of sound presents itself in one-on-one interactions between the listener and the artwork as well. Here, sound acts both as the creative product of the participant's actions and as a feedback mechanism, guiding them through the work's affordances and encouraging exploration. Finally, sound facilitates immersion and refocuses the participants' perception from vision to listening, creating a seamless continuity between their actions, aesthetic experience and meaning-making.

The categorisation of participatory sound art into three environment types in the second section reflects the different qualities of sound propagation in these environments. This in turn stipulates the similarities in the kinds of interactions afforded to the participants. Sound art in local environments relies on the continuity of its spatial structure and immediacy and corporeality of its sound-producing and listening mechanisms to encourage the participants to interact with the works (physically) and each other (socially). Networked sound art, on the other hand, employs the network's ability to connect spaces and actors over various barriers, both physical and institutional, to create participatory structures that would be impossible in local environments, for example, due to entry barriers. Augmented environments introduce a new sonic layer to the existing sites, enhancing the participants' perception and making them engage deeper with the site and its natural, cultural and social aspects.

There is however a significant interaction between universal and environment-specific affordances and the ways they manifest themselves. Affordance for creativity is realised differently depending on whether participants use their voices or their own sounds or have to learn the sonic capabilities and interfaces of the artwork first. Technological literacy in itself can act as a constraint (see Norman 2013) on participation and creativity, as unfamiliarity with a piece of technology may lead to misreading the work's possibilities or anxiety about expressing oneself in an unknown medium.

However, this same unfamiliarity may enhance exploratory and experimental behaviours. Low-tech works in local environments, such as the Baschets' sculptures, expose their inner workings to the participants. The participants' exploration of and experimentation with such works may have a goal of learning its sonic capabilities and eventually develop into an expressive and deliberate performance. On the other hand, an opaquer technology in networked or augmented environments may, intentionally or not, obfuscate the connection between the participants' actions and their sonic result. In *#tweetscapes*, complex algorithms used to transform posts into sounds make it impossible for the participants to aim for a specific sonority. In such cases, curiosity rather than expression may become the main driving force for participation.

The technological underpinnings of the artwork furthermore influence how and amongst whom the connections are established, affecting the affordance for connectivity. Where in local, physical environments it is the result of sound filling the space and prompting a reaction from the others, like LaBelle (2015) notes, things get more complicated with the introduction of networks. On the one hand, works like *Auracle* allow in principle random strangers to join collective soundmaking sessions on a whim. On the other hand, works like *#tweetscapes* may separate soundmaking and social connections into different streams (or even different platforms in this particular case), so sound becomes more of an excuse to connect than a connecting medium. Similarly, as Seth Kim-Cohen (2009) notes, unusual behaviours of the participants experiencing augmented sound environments—e.g., Kubisch's *Electrical Walks*—may prompt chance encounters with passers-by not participating in the artwork, extending the connectivity beyond its context and beyond the shared listening experience.

References

Azuma, Ronald, Yohan Baillot, Reinhold Behringer, Steven Feiner, and Simon Julier. 2001. Recent advances in augmented reality. *IEEE Computer Graphics and Applications* 21: 34–47.

Barbosa, Álvaro. 2003. Displaced soundscapes: A survey of network systems for music and sonic art creation. *Leonardo Music Journal* 13: 53–59.

Baschet, François, and Bernard Baschet. 1987. Sound sculpture: Sounds, shapes, public participation, education. *Leonardo* 20: 107–114.

Born, Georgina. 2019. On nonhuman sound: Sound as relation. In *Sound objects*, ed. Rey Chow and James Steintrager, 185–208. Durham, NC: Duke University Press.

Carmigniani, Julie, and Borko Furht. 2011. Augmented reality: An overview. In *Handbook of augmented reality*, ed. Borko Furht, 3–46. New York: Springer.
Caudell, Thomas P., and David W. Mizell. 1992. Augmented reality: An application of heads-up display technology to manual manufacturing processes. In *Proceedings of the twenty-fifth Hawaii international conference on system sciences*, 659–669. Kauai, HI: IEEE.
Collins, Karen. 2013. *Playing with sound: A theory of interacting with sound and music in video games*. Cambridge, MA: MIT Press.
Dewey, John. 1980 [1934]. *Art as experience*. New York: Perigee Books.
Fedorova, Ksenia. 2016. Sound cartographies and navigation art: In search of the sublime. *Leonardo Electronic Almanac* 21: 44–59.
Föllmer, Golo. 1999. Klangorganisation im öffentlichen Raum. In *Klangkunst. Tönende Objekte und klingende Räume*, ed. Helga de la Motte-Haber, 191–227. Laaber: Laaber-Verlag.
Graham, Beryl. 2010. What kind of participative system? Critical vocabularies from new media art. In *The "do-it-yourself" artwork: Participation from Fluxus to new media*, ed. Anna Dezeuze, 281–305. Manchester and New York: Manchester University Press.
Keylin, Vadim. 2019. Medialities of participation in sound art. In *Cultures of participation: Arts, digital media and cultural institutions*, ed. Birgit Eriksson, Carsten Stage, and Bjarki Valtýsson, 129–146. New York: Routledge.
———. 2020. Crash, boom, bang: Affordances for participation in sound art. *SoundEffects* 9: 98–115. https://doi.org/10.7146/se.v9i1.118243.
Kim-Cohen, Seth. 2009. *In the blink of an ear: Toward a non-cochlear sonic art*. New York and London: Continuum.
LaBelle, Brandon. 2015. *Background noise: Perspectives on sound art*. 2nd ed. New York: Bloomsbury.
Norman, Donald A. 2013. *The design of everyday things: Revised and expanded edition*. London: Hachette UK.
Polli, Andrea. 2017. Soundwalking, sonification and activism. In *Routledge companion to sounding art*, ed. Marcel Cobussen, Vincent Meelberg, and Barry Truax, 81–91. Abingdon: Routledge.
Schroeder, Franziska, and Pedro Rebelo. 2017. Distributed sounding art: Practices in distributing sound. In *Routledge companion to sounding art*, ed. Marcel Cobussen, Vincent Meelberg, and Barry Truax, 439-450. Abingdon: Routledge.
Schulze, Holger. 2018. *The sonic persona: An anthropology of sound*. London: Bloomsbury.
Tanaka, Atau. 2018. Prométhée Numérique Frankensteins Netz. June 20.
Truax, Barry. 1984. *Acoustic communication*. Norwood, NJ: Ablex Publishing Corporation.

CHAPTER 5

Perspectives

Abstract While Chap. 4 discusses the material agencies of sound artworks, this chapter turns to creative agencies and perspectives of the human actors involved in such artworks—artists and participants. Its central theoretical device G.H. Mead's notion of perspective—the way one's perception of their immediate environment is structured by their intention to act in certain ways. The chapter adopts creativity psychologist Vlad Glaveanu's view on perspective and taking new perspectives as a necessary condition for creative acts. The chapter discusses the process and mechanisms of perspective-taking in participatory sound art through two qualitative case studies: Katrine Faber's performance *Let Us Sing Your Place* and Benoît Maubrey's sculptures *Obelisk* and *Speakers Arena*. It then contextualises the findings of the case studies by discussing, on the one hand, the sound artists' statements and theoretical works on participation, and on the other hand ethnomusicological and sociological studies of participatory music. Examining the role of the artists, the chapter focuses on how the delegation of agency from the author of the participatory sound artwork to its audiences is negotiated and mediated by the artwork's materialities. It investigates the reasons sound artists introduce participation into their works and their methods of expressing their creativity through participation. At the same time, it explores how the participants conceptualise

© The Author(s), under exclusive license to Springer Nature
Singapore Pte Ltd. 2023
V. Keylin, *Participatory Sound Art*, Palgrave Studies in Sound,
https://doi.org/10.1007/978-981-99-6357-7_5

their experience of the artwork, how they translate this conceptualisation into actions and how they relate it to their experiences in a broader social context.

Keywords Agency • Creativity • Benoît Maubrey • Katrine Faber

5.1 Creative Agency[1]

The question of creative agency has long been dominating the discussions of both participatory art and sound art independently of each other. Already aleatoric music—the phenomenon that inspired Umberto Eco's (1989) poetics of the open work—has raised concerns with whether "the liberation of sound" means the enslavement of "composer, performer, and listener alike", as the chance operations come to override human creativity (Taruskin 2010, 62). Not surprisingly, participatory art proper is likewise often met with critique of its ethical ambivalence towards the issues of "labour, exploitation and custodianship" (Bala 2018, 85). At the same time, both participatory art and sound art have been criticised for their avoidance of authorship, leaving them in the eyes and ears of the critics aesthetically and politically impotent (see, e.g., Kim-Cohen 2009; Bishop 2012). Finally, a strong speculative realist trend in recent aesthetics brings attention to the non-human agencies of artworks and materialities that compose them (Felski 2017).

On the other hand, as I discussed in Chap. 3, participation is contingent. It is because participatory art sacrifices its autonomy that it becomes entrenched in its social context, necessarily including its site, its institutional framing, but also the participants themselves, their circumstances and the ways they choose to engage with what the artists propose. The participants' perspectives (in the Meadian sense—i.e., their action-orientations) and the process of taking the perspectives of others that Vlad Glaveanu (2015) writes about become particularly important to the analysis of creative exchanges taking place in participatory sound artworks.

---

[1] The material of Sects. 5.1–5.3 has previously appeared in: Keylin, Vadim. 2023. Creative Agencies in Participatory Sound Art: Two Case Studies. *Organised Sound* 28 (1): 13–24. https://doi.org/10.1017/S1355771822000085. The text has been edited for the purposes of this book.

This chapter's thematic focus makes it diverge in its approach from the rest of the book. As perspectives are unique to their holders—and, in case of participatory art, highly contingent and situational—it would not be possible to discuss them using only analyses of the artworks' materialities and structures. Thus, this chapter first details two qualitative case studies that I conducted using ethnographic observations and interviews to gain insight into the ways the artists and participants exercise their creative agencies in participatory sound art. I then contextualise these empirical findings within a broader review of the sound artists' own writings on participation.

The two practices that formed the basis of my case studies are Benoît Maubrey's *Speaker Sculptures* and Katrine Faber's performance *Let Us Sing Your Place*. Maubrey's large-scale interactive sculptures built of repurposed loudspeakers have already been discussed in the previous chapter. For my observations and interviews, I chose two, *Obelisk* and *Speakers Arena* (both 2019), installed in the public spaces of Potsdam and Berlin respectively. In Faber's performance, which I attended on two different occasions in 2019, audience members took turns describing places that they hold dear—remembered, longed for or dreamt up—and their soundscapes. The rest of the audience would then try to recreate these soundscapes with their voices.

These two practices represent two antithetical but complementary approaches to participation in sound art. One is an indoor performance with minimal technological setup and a ritualistic sensibility. The other is a public space installation relying on an extensive technological apparatus. Thus, while these two approaches do not exhaust the field of possibilities for sonic participation, they provide an important starting point to open the discussion on creative agency and perspective in participatory sound art.

5.2 Katrine Faber: *Let Us Sing Your Place*

Let Us Sing Your Place is a participatory performance with an elegantly simple cycle at its core. One of the audience members volunteers to describe a place that has an importance to them, then the rest improvise a one-minute soundscape of that place with their voices. This cycle continues for as long as the timeframe of the performance allows. The staging is decidedly minimalistic to foreground this interaction. The audience is arranged in a circle, facing a solitary chair at its centre that is reserved for the person sharing their place. Faber controls the temporality of the performance, marking the beginning and end of each singing segment with a "ding" on crotales, and joins the impromptu choir as one of the voices, but otherwise does not interfere in the process. No other set decorations, costumes or props are present.

Let Us Sing Your Place is part of Faber's larger project *Singing Our Place*, which has so far resulted in several productions by her theatre company *Teater Viva* (The Camp, 2015; Tales from the Trash, 2017, and others) and a festival of music and performance art in Aarhus, Denmark, in 2019. The initial inspiration came from the United Nations' Sustainable Development Goals programme and the Paris Climate Summit in 2015. Faber's ambition was "to investigate what it means to be human within a particular environment, to be connected or not to nature, both the nature around you and the nature of your body", relating the "stories about global climate change to the individual's perception of place and nature" (Faber 2019, 8–9).

For the purposes of this study, I have attended *Let Us Sing Your Place* twice in Denmark: first, at *Sjón* anthropological film festival in Copenhagen in March 2019; second, at the *Singing Our Place* festival of vocal music and performance art in Aarhus in June of the same year.[2] Different disciplinary and thematic framings of the two events attracted tangibly different audiences. *Sjón*'s audience was smaller in size (approximately 20–25 people) and consisted of mostly younger people of all genders. The audience at *Singing Our Place* was larger (45–50 people), predominantly female or female-presenting, had more age diversity, and included a number of professional and amateur musicians. I interviewed three of *Sjón*'s attendees and six more at Singing Our Place. Despite the small size, this sample covers a range of participation strategies, including those who volunteered to describe a place as well as those who did not, and those who participated in singing as well as those who did not.

5.2.1 Inviting Noises

Participatory art requires the participants to take the perspectives of both *the* artist—to appreciate artistic intent—and *an* artist—to assume creative agency delegated to them. But since established protocols and conventions of participation do not exist, these perspectives need to be

---

[2] I have also had previous experience with the performance, attending it during the Sound Forms symposium in Copenhagen in October 2018.

communicated to the participants in some way. In other words, perspectives being action-orientations, the participants need to be oriented, first, to act (rather than receive); and second, to act in an appropriate way. Theatre scholar Gareth White (2013) calls this process "invitation". Invitation need not be explicit—it can operate as a kind of social affordance invoking creativity through, for instance, appealing to stable cultural forms and conventions—but it is crucial for the contract between the artist and the participants.

In a work like *Let Us Sing Your Place*, where both the "scripts" (descriptions of places) and vocal performances are created by the participants, invitation becomes the primary locus of artist's agency, and at the same time, responsibility:

> I nearly thought it was too simple. [...] Can you call this a performance? Because, as you say, it's mostly created with the people. But yes, I think you can call it a performance and I think it's not so easy-peasy thing to do. Because in this performance, I must use all my experience as an actress, as a performer, and as improviser myself, and as a psychotherapist actually—also as a teacher [...]—to have this respect [for the participants], so you don't start to invade people. (Katrine Faber in interview with the author, August 9, 2019)

Invitation in *Let Us Sing Your Place* takes the form of an introductory part that Faber performs solo, aided by a real-time sampler, and that can take up to a half of performance's allotted time. It includes vocal improvisations, spoken comments on the theme and structure of the performance, and some vocal exercises for the audience. Faber also introduces a place and a soundscape of her own that she first sings herself with the sampler, then asks the audience to sing with her.

Reflecting on the composite character of this introduction, Faber notes:

> I'm trying to open the space of sounding, so they're somehow aware of the possibilities that you can use all kinds of sounds. And then I know by experience—when I was younger, sometimes I insisted I didn't want to use words [...] But I learned that it's good to just say a little bit about—what are we doing and why, so people relax a little bit more. [...] Knowing here that in a moment I will invite the people to participate themselves, I don't want to scare them, I want them to feel safe. [However,] it's also about not to say too much because it's not to start to be the guide, to give the space—to say,

I should not perform this, I open the space to the creativity of the group. (Interview with the author, August 9, 2019)

In other words, a significant part of the artist's perspective in *Let Us Sing Your Place* and of its contract of participation is communicated to the audience through non-verbal and sonic means. Faber's professed goal is to create an inviting sound that would relax the audience and make them feel safe. Conventionally, safety and relaxation are associated with harmonious, melodic and not overly complicated or emotionally charged sounds, as demonstrated by Muzak and various other sonic mood control systems (see, e.g., Lanza, 2016). However, Faber's approach is exactly the opposite:

> I try to go in there, and be a little ugly myself, and be very human, not perfect. I'm not delivering a beautiful performance, I'm not singing opera to impress. […] I try to create this atmosphere that—this is not about being perfect, or good, or fantastic. (Interview with the author, August 9, 2019)

As Chris Tonelli (2016, 2) argues, vocal performances that do not conform to the "dominant forms of singing wherein melody and the production of 'pure' pitch content predominate" often provoke an ableist reaction in the audience. In other words, the perspective of a typical Western concertgoer is shaped by established cultural conventions, which impel the listener to judge the artist on their virtuosity and technical skill (expected to exceed the abilities of a layperson). An experimental musician's palette of noisy, ostensibly mundane and ordinary sounds defies these conventions and is therefore often judged as lack of ability and self-awareness. The sonic palette that Faber uses in her introduction—and that the participants will get to use themselves thereafter—consists of sighs, coughs, whispers, yells and the like. Such sounds would probably be rated as outrageous in a vocal music concert—unless its audience consists of connoisseurs of extended vocal techniques. However, in the context of *Let Us Sing Your Place*, it is the lack of virtuosity and skill, of conventionally understood beauty, and the unfamiliarity of the sounds that are somehow soothing and inviting to the audience.

This acceptance is the result of how two perspectives are reconciled in *Let Us Sing Your Place*: those of a listener and a participant. The audience of the performance are both listeners and participants. Their potential reluctance to participate stems from the same assumed expectation that they will be judged on their technical skills. In rejecting virtuosity in her vocal performance, Faber gives up her power to judge the participants, levelling the playing field and assuaging the audience's anxiety. Her implicit invitation does not appeal to the participants' familiarity with cultural conventions, as in White's theory; on the contrary, Faber achieves her desired goal by breaking away from them. At the same time, by accepting this contract of non-judgement, the participants give up their own orientation to judge, allowing themselves to appreciate the "unmusical" sounds aesthetically. Taking a new perspective does not just make "previously unperceived affordances salient" (Glaveanu 2015, 170)—which it also does with regard to participants' own voices—but retunes their perception and aesthetic sensibility as well. As I will discuss in the following sections, this new sensibility emerges both in the participants' singing strategies and in their self-assessment of their performance.

5.2.2 How Do You Sing a Place?

The participant perspective makes the audience appreciate "unmusical" sounds as a medium for their creativity—but leaves the specific palette of these sounds intentionally open. In both performances I observed, the participants used several similar strategies of making sound, despite the differences in audience composition.

Some of these strategies directly corresponded to the notions of R.M. Schafer's (1993) soundscape theory. At both events, I heard the majority of the participants producing some kind of drones: muted, sustained tones or sibilant noises imitating the sounds of winds and waves or unidentifiable hums. While there might be a psychological explanation for this—such sounds allow one to fade into the background, to participate without putting themselves into the spotlight—this also correlates well with the structure of natural soundscapes. Schafer (1993, 9–10) called the various drones present in an acoustic environment "keynote sounds", as they glue the soundscape together and create a backdrop against which other sounds ("signals") attain their meaning.

The second strategy was imitating immediately recognisable, iconic sounds: animal and bird calls, human speech and non-verbal exclamations, artificial noises. In a natural soundscape, these would qualify as signals. However, in the context of *Let Us Sing Your Place* they are closer to "soundmarks"—sounds that give an acoustic environment its unique character (Schafer 1993, 10)—as they relate directly to the way in which a place was described and thus hold particular importance to its soundscape.

Two other strategies do not have direct correlates in natural soundscapes. Some sounds I have heard in both performances stood out against the drones but had an abstract character. At times they were closer to traditional singing, at times more experimental, but their implied sources were not immediately recognisable. These might be the participants' failures to voice soundmarks, but they may also represent a more impressionistic approach to singing a soundscape, an attempt to express its mood rather than literal sound.

Finally, only at the *Sjón* performance have I observed the phenomenon of "chain reactions"—when a participant would come up with a new soundmark (e.g., a particular birdcall), which would then be copied by more and more people until a saturation point is reached. Interestingly, none of the people I interviewed said they had been intentionally copying others during the performance.[3] On the contrary, most participants at both events claimed they had been aiming for variety and completeness of the soundscape.

These singing strategies are the most direct expression of the participants' creativity in *Let Us Sing Your Place*, and they make explicit the process of perspective-taking that Glaveanu (2015) talks about. In a sense, this process forms the core of the performance's dramaturgy. The participants have to imagine themselves inside soundscapes conjured by their peers and partake in the other's hearing perspective. This is further reinforced by the performance's spatial arrangement: the participant who describes a place sits in the centre and the singers stand peripherally.

The reason these four singing strategies are so prominent can be attributed to the relational and fluid character of the singers' perspectives. They are built from four principal sources—Faber's invitation, the description of the place and its soundscape, the participants' past listening experiences and their non-verbal exchange with each other in the process of singing—glued together by the goal of reimagining and recreating a soundscape.

On the one hand, the participants only have a short description to work from, so they have to relate it to their past experiences of similar soundscapes and sounding objects, creating a composite perspective. On the other hand, they also need to translate it into a vocal action, reassessing the affordances of their voices and their bodies in the light of how they can

---

[3] This may have been due to the small sample.

contribute to the re-creation of this soundscape. Finally, they have to work as a group and coordinate with each other, aiming for a complete acoustic image, without any protocols or agreements established beforehand. Taken together, these factors lead to the participants dissociating their vocal performance from the conventional singing practices and to "giving voice" to a place or "getting [the] place alive with sound", as one of my interviewees put it, instead.

It is interesting to compare the singing strategies in soundscape segments with the last part of the performance where Faber asks the audience to sing the sound of the future. In this case, there is no soundscape description to work from, no past experiences to relate to and no necessity to coordinate with each other. As a result, the dissociation from singing does not happen. In both cases I have observed, the sound of the future ended up being louder and more musical and impressionistic.

5.2.3 Sound, Voice, Singing

> It was sound more than singing. I was mostly making other sounds, like birds.

This quotation from one of my interviewees is perhaps the most direct expression of the sentiment, shared by many participants. It clearly demonstrates a move away from the concertgoer's perspective. Even though the title of the performance is *Let Us* Sing *Your Place*, my respondents often avoided describing their actions as "singing", using variations of "making sound" or "giving sound" instead. In many cases, these expressions were explicitly or implicitly associated with rejecting not only sonic but also social conventions of music performance—the expectations to show off their skill and be judged aesthetically:

> It was very personal in some ways because you can choose by yourself which kind of sound to make, and nobody says which is good or not, every sound could be. (Anonymous participant in interview with the author, June 6, 2019)
>
> I was standing there, in this room, being sure that nobody made their sound to get forward on the stage and being listened to [...] and that was very beautiful, and very different from normal concert or so. At least at a normal concert you can't be sure if the artist is trying to show himself. (Anonymous participant in interview with the author, June 6, 2019)

The hesitance to show off might be attributed to a general reluctance of the participants in such projects to take the spotlight. Indeed, some of the people I talked to admitted to being shy or having issues with public speaking and performing. However, some of the participants at *Singing Our Place* were professional singers and thus less likely to have stage anxiety. Moreover, their training and professional experience would have made the expectation to show off their skill and be judged aesthetically an intrinsic part of their perspectives, yet they were even more determined to break away from the traditional modes of performing:

> You have to actually rid … empty your head from all the things you've learnt—what's right and wrong, and stuff like that, so you have to be in another … think in another way. (Anonymous participant in interview with the author, June 6, 2019)
> I tried to get the story out of my head and into my body and emotions. And then two of the times I just felt like giving no sound, just receiving and being curious of the other, of the audiences" pictures and sounds. (Anonymous participant in interview with the author, June 6, 2019)

In other words, in the participants' perspective, vocal sounds become dissociated from the normative practice of singing, which removes the frame of reference for aesthetic judgement, whether directed at others or oneself. In the absence of such a frame, virtuosic, self-expression-focused performance becomes impossible, opening the space up for more altruistic approaches to creativity. In that sense, the participants' behaviour and their perspectives in *Let Us Sing Your Place* unsettle not only the notion of singing but also that of the voice itself.

As Amanda Weidman (2015, 233) notes, the voice in Western culture has been traditionally seen "as [a] guarantor of truth and self-presence, from which springs the familiar idea that the voice expresses self and identity and that agency consists in having a voice". Faber frames her performance in similar terms: "this is also about that we have to remember—we all have a voice, we all have an importance", although noting that "maybe [we] also have a responsibility to use our voices […] for all other living things" (Interview with the author; August 9, 2019).

However, what characterises the participants' action-orientations in *Let Us Sing Your Place* is precisely the lack of self-expression—the voice is freely given away, willingly subjected to execute the other's perspective. Moreover, the participants decided whether their place was worth sharing—whether it would be "a funny thing to do for the others" or not—in a similarly altruistic way.

The association between voice and authenticity is also questioned, as it is used for imitation rather than self-expression—for mimicking the elements of a natural soundscape—and is shaped by other voices. The sonic content of the participants' singing emphasises what Roland Barthes (1977) called "the grain of the voice"—its corporeality and imperfection—yet instead of attesting to one's identity, it becomes infinitely malleable in an altruistic gesture of subordinating one's voice to the Other and the others.

5.3 BENOÎT MAUBREY: *SPEAKER SCULPTURES*

My second case study is based on two of Benoît Maubrey's *Speaker Sculptures*—*Obelisk* and *Speakers Arena*. *Obelisk* was commissioned by the *Intersonanzen* festival for new music. It was installed in the middle of Platz der Einheit public park in Potsdam from May 30 to June 5, 2019. *Speakers Arena* was independently produced by the *Zwitschermachine* gallery. It occupied a spot in a small square on Pallasstrasse in Berlin, next to the *Pallasseum* housing complex, from July 1 to October 27, 2019. At each sculpture, I have conducted observations over five days starting from the opening and interviewing the participants on-site. Owing to extended temporality of the works, my sample here is slightly larger than in the case of *Let Us Sing Your Place*, with fourteen interviews collected across two works.

Both *Obelisk* and *Speakers Arena* were built of 320 active loudspeakers composed into the shape of a stella (*Obelisk*) and an amphitheatre (*Arena*) respectively and allowed the participants to interact with them in several ways. The participants could use a phone number to call the sculpture and have their call broadcast by it in real time, connect their smartphones via Bluetooth or a cable to play their music and other sounds or use an on-site microphone. Additionally, *Speakers Arena* would sonify via a text-to-speech software any Twitter post that was marked with the hashtag #speakersarena.

5.3.1 *Non-cochlear Musicking*

Speaker Sculptures are intermedia artworks that operate across two different media: visual (sculptural) and sonic. The former is stable and remains largely unchanged by the acts of participation (unless we take this category to include vandalism);[4] the latter, on the other hand, is fully created by the participants. The artist's influence on *Speaker Sculptures*' sound is limited to designing technological affordances of the sculpture—such as ways of connection (Bluetooth, phone lines, Twitter), the number of simultaneous interactions, or the possible time limit on interactions. Thus, the creative agencies of the artist and the participants are clearly split along the sculptural-sonic lines. Indeed, according to Maubrey, what drives his sound sculpture practice is not an interest in music or sound aesthetics, but the desire to work in outdoor spaces and shape them with sound, using it as a sort of sculptural material:

> I got involved in music because I wanted to work outdoors, not because I wanted to make music. Because I wasn't making music. I don't know any notes, I can't write any notes. And that's what my main thing is, I don't care about improvisational music or any of that kind of stuff, I just care about rooms and spaces, outdoor spaces, and how to make the air vibrate inside them, and build structures so that they can exist outdoors. […] But I'm interested in this kind of interaction, in letting the people say what they want to say. […] You can still say you're composing because you set up the system and you let the people talk. I mean, I'm sure that works also in the way of John Cage, about letting sounds happen as opposed to composing yourself. (Interview with the author, August 18, 2018)

Glaveanu (2015, 168) notes that a perspective "effectively 'bridge[s]' difference by relating two previously separate positions", one new and one familiar. The quotation above reveals Maubrey's artistic perspective to extend from the position of a sculptor, perhaps also in the figurative sense of Joseph Beuys' (1974) "social sculpture", towards that of a composer or a soundmaker. This perspective highlights material rather than aesthetic affordances of sound: its ability to "sculpt" the air, to create and arrange invisible volumes through vibration. Similarly, participation itself becomes an affordance for generating sound—but also for sculpting a social situation in a way that evokes playful Dadaist noise practices. It is aimed at upsetting the order of the everyday through unrestricted and undirected soundmaking, "making a small revolution in the street", as Maubrey puts it. This playfulness is shared by the participants as well, with some likening

---

[4] In some cases, however, the creation of the sculpture may be influenced by participatory processes. For example, an earlier version of *Obelisk* in Cairo (2018) was assembled from loudspeakers and boomboxes provided by the city's residents.

the sculpture to a playground to explore and experiment with, either for themselves or for their kids.

This approach to sound evokes Seth Kim-Cohen's (2009) notion of non-cochlear sound art. Comparing sound art to contemporary visual—though "non-retinal" (Kim-Cohen 2009, xxi)—art, he criticises the former's alleged indulgence in the perceptual and sensory aspects of sound, which he traces to John Cage's (1961, 10) call to "let sounds be themselves". Kim-Cohen calls instead for a kind of sound art that would rethink sound and auditory practices from a poststructuralist perspective, as performative and discursively framed.

At first glance, *Speaker Sculptures* can be described as non-cochlear sound artworks. As discussed above, for Maubrey, sound is primarily a means for sculpting physical and social space—a goal which takes precedence over how exactly his sculptures sound. But at the same time, this non-cochlear quality is achieved precisely by letting sounds happen through participation. Moreover, participation and liberation of sonic expression are crucial for the political and discursive functioning of *Speaker Sculptures*. Maubrey uses the metaphor of Speakers' Corner in London's Hyde Park to describe his work—a place historically reserved for free speech and self-expression.

The participants themselves approach their soundmaking with *Speaker Sculptures* largely in non-cochlear manner. The three kinds of interaction that I have observed most frequently also prioritise performative gestures over sonic content. First, especially in case of *Obelisk*, the passers-by often stopped by the sculpture only for a couple of seconds to say or sing a few short phrases into the microphone before moving on. Second, some people brought their children to the sculptures to sing, recite a poem or just play around. Finally, and most frequently, the participants simply played some music from the smartphones—typically described as their favourite music or whatever they had in their playlist. Occasionally, some of the approaches were mixed together—for example, one couple played some electronic music tracks produced by their adult son.

I am not arguing that sonic content of the participants' actions was irrelevant. On the contrary, their favourite music, their children's creativity, their own singing clearly held importance to them. The intention to have a listening experience was a necessary part of their participant perspectives. However, as listening experiences, these interactions did not radically differ in their sonic quality from the participants' everyday listening practices. The acoustic characteristics of *Speaker Sculptures* are different from those of a consumer sound system, but not different enough to alter the sounds coming through them in fundamental ways. It is the context of participation—the fact of interacting with this particular sculpture in this particular time and space and its mediation of the musicking act—that makes it meaningful.

5.3.2 Sound Art, Mediation, Participation

According to Glaveanu (2013, 2015), a creative act is necessarily mediated by the affordances of its material and social conditions. Furthermore, this mediation is central to the cycle of perspective-taking: acting upon these affordances reorients the actor's perspective, revealing previously unperceived affordances. In actor-network theory, mediation is also the means by which non-human actors express their agency. According to Bruno Latour (1994), they do so by modifying—mediating—human acts, their goals or their expressions—in other words, their perspectives. While Glaveanu's concern lies primarily with human creative agency, this process opens up the possibility of looking into non-human agencies and their role in participatory creativity.

At the same time, as discussed above, mediation—both the process and the experience—forms the core of the participants' perspectives when interacting with *Speaker Sculptures*. It makes sense then to examine the role of mediation, non-human agencies and their influence on the artist's and the audience's perspectives in more detail.

On the technological level, mediation affects the agencies and perspectives of both the participants and the artist. As Maubrey notes, his creative development largely paralleled that of audio and interactive technologies, with *Speaker Sculptures* attaining new ways of interactions as technological means became available:

> That's also a very interesting phenomenon, that the electronics has moved along with me—or I'm just following the electronics. [...] Before that, it didn't exist, all the electronics—now electronics is just a part of society. So, it's also normal - not just normal - that artists also adapt and use new tools, but also why not? Here's electronics, what is it supposed to do? Oh, it's for communication, right. So why not build a sculpture out of it? (Interview with the author, August 18, 2018)

On the participants' side, the technologies play a somewhat ambiguous role, both affording participation and constraining it. On the one hand, they provide the means for the participants to interact with the sculptures. On the other, for some, they also hindered possible interactions, be it due to lack of technological literacy, habits or simply anxiety:

> I used it via Bluetooth because I think Bluetooth is a nice piece to be interacting with it, yeah. ... And I don't trust [phone] numbers. That's not my thing. There are some reasons for that—I need to know, need to see who I'm talking to. (Anonymous participant in interview with the author, July 1, 2019)

At the same time, mediational entities operate on different levels of emergence. Even though composed of many different technologies and materialities, a *Speaker Sculpture* as a whole functions as a singular mediator via a mechanism that Latour (1994) calls blackboxing. Since the artist is absent at the site of *Speaker Sculptures*, the work mediates his own creative agency with regard to the participants. It essentially serves as an invitation—a way of inducing a participant perspective in the audience, which in this case amounts to legitimising sonic practices that do not conform to the everyday auditory protocols of public spaces.

Many participants admitted that they would not normally play their music or sing in public but felt empowered to do so in the context of the artwork. In other words, public soundmaking was not in their everyday perspectives, but entered their perspectives as participants through the sculpture's mediation:

> I don't like it when people take their boomboxes or smartphone music and play it out loud. I don't like it in a park or something like that but here it's cool. Because it's a place where you can go and play some music. (Anonymous participant in interview with the author, July 2, 2019)

Furthermore, mediation does not stop with the sculpture itself. As Sanne Krogh Groth and Kristine Samson (2017) argue, sound artworks necessarily become entangled in their spatial and social context, operating as situations rather than works, and are impossible to separate from their contingencies. For *Speaker Sculptures*, these contingencies include the work's embeddedness in specific sites, their temporalities and curatorial framings. Because of the difference in materialities and contexts between

Obelisk and *Speakers Arena*, the participants' perspectives and their behaviour also differed significantly between the two cases.

Obelisk was installed in the middle of a public park, at the crossing of two busy walkways. A festival worker was stationed nearby each day, actively inviting the passers-by to participate and explaining to them the way the sculpture operated. Additionally, in absence of participants, the festival workers often played their own music, possibly as a means of implicit invitation. All this resulted in most of the participant interactions being brief—most only played one or two songs, or said or sang a few phrases into the microphone. On the other hand, *Speakers Arena* was situated in a relatively quiet site for several months, largely unattended, with the instructions printed on a poster handing nearby. Most importantly, the sculpture made in the shape of an amphitheatre had seating rows embedded into it. Accordingly, on average, the participants spent significantly longer times with the sculpture, up to several hours. These differences show the reciprocity of the relationship between affordances of the artwork and the participants' perspectives, as they inform one another.

Finally, the participants' perspectives are also at least partly mediated even before interacting with the sculpture, which is evident in the sonic content of such interactions. In my observations, it was relatively rare that the participants used their voices directly (apart from the brief on-the-go interactions mentioned above), be it through the microphone or the phone lines—most played music from their smartphones. When asked why not, most of the time they replied they had nothing to say or that they were not singers. Those who did sing (or in one case, whistle) did so in a karaoke fashion, singing to a simultaneously played track.

Here it is instructive to draw a comparison between *Speaker Sculptures* and *Let Us Sing Your Place*. Both works unsettle the connection between voice and identity or agency but do so in opposite ways. In *Let Us Sing Your Place*, participants use their voices for goals that have little to do with self-expression. In *Speaker Sculptures*, conversely, participants do self-express sonically, but prefer to use means other than voice for that, building their identities and perspectives through reference to other sonic artefacts.

To sum up, the sound of *Speaker Sculptures* is a product of a complex interplay of agencies, perspectives and materialities mediating and transforming each other. The artist exercises his agency by initiating a situation that legitimises public soundmaking and delimits the field of sonic possibilities through the artwork's affordances. These affordances, together with the artwork's curatorial framing and its embeddedness in a particular site and socio-cultural context, influence the participants' perspectives, making various interactions and behaviours more or less likely to occur. Finally, sonic content is then supplied by the participants but influenced by a number of external mediators and media.

However, as discussed in the previous chapter, the mediational networks—and thereby the process of perspective-taking—arguably extend beyond the moment of soundmaking, in the participants' documenting their experience and publishing it on social media for the secondary audiences. It is especially tangible in the case of *Speakers Arena*, which is directly connected to Twitter by way of the #speakersarena hashtag.

On the one hand, posts marked with this hashtag both trigger an interaction with the sculpture and memorialise that interaction at the same time. They remain on the social network long after the sculpture is uninstalled from its physical spot. They extend its temporality, but they also extend its public reach. The statements in these posts are performed at the same time in the public space of the sculpture's site and in the public sphere of social media. While not reflecting the way these statements sounded, they attest to the fact that they sounded and were heard.

On the other hand, contemporary digital mobile technologies provide an easy way to document the sound of *Speaker Sculptures* as well. While not a part of the artwork as designed, mobile technologies and social media are a necessary part of most participants' lives and their perspectives. In the entanglement of agencies, materialities and mediation that is a sound art situation they become largely inseparable from the aesthetic experience and provide further ways for the participants to exercise their creativity.

Such dynamic entanglement between the on-site functioning of the sculpture and its social media documentation extends the acoustic space of the artwork, making its sounds and soundmaking affordances available across distances. What is important, however, is that it is not a part of the artwork's design but is entirely facilitated by the participants. In other words, the balance of agencies gets reversed in this case, with the participants acting as mediators of the sculpture's sound.

5.4 Perspectives on Participation

5.4.1 "Catalyser of Sound Activity": Artists

Reflecting on his pioneering participatory radio works of the 1960s, Max Neuhaus (1994, n.p.) remarked that in doing so he wanted "to move beyond [being a musician] and beyond being a composer, *into the idea of being a catalyser of sound activity*" (emphasis mine). My case studies of *Let Us Sing Your Place* and *Speaker Sculptures* have shown the centrality of this idea for the artists' perspectives in participatory sound art. Both Faber and Maubrey admit that their artistic goals lie outside of the actual sonorities of their works: in engaging the site and the environment for Maubrey ("making the air vibrate"), and in being (co-)present and facilitating connections for Faber. In a sense, this perspective aligns with Alan Licht's (2019) remark that a sound artist is more of a listener than a soundmaker. However, it also reveals a different modality of being a listener for a sound artist—listening *to* the public rather than *sharing the artist's own* listening with them.

A cursory look at the writings and interviews of other sound artists reveals a similar attitude: one of composing situations where the audience's sonic creativity could unfold rather than composing sound. Tellingly, the artist might not even like what they hear, as this quote from the Baschet brothers reveals—demonstrating an ironic reversal of positions between the artists and the audiences regarding "non-musical" sounds:

> Philosophically, we are happy when the public enjoys our exhibitions. And, as a general rule, it does.
> Musically, the result is often a sheer disaster. If one puts a small child in front of a piano, the child will pound on it as heavily as possible: "I make noise, therefore I exist". If one puts an adult in front of a sound sculpture and hands the adult a mallet, the same thing will happen: "I make noise". But I am sure that in both cases the hyperactivity stems from the pleasure of discovering. Next time both child and adult will behave better. It is a matter of education. (Baschet and Baschet 1987, 110)

Nevertheless, the Baschets, like many other creators of participatory sound art, acknowledge that the importance of unleashing the creativity of their publics outweighs the disagreement over the sonic result.

Furthermore, for many sound artists, this "sound activity" may have explicitly political rather than purely aesthetic goals, relying on the particular mediality of sound to avoid the "didactical provocation" (Kester 2011, 9) and the associated hierarchisation. For example, Jeremy Woodruff (2020) maintains that a sound practice that would transcend the purely aesthetic considerations and engage with social relationships should necessarily be participatory. A social sensibility, according to Woodruff, should emerge on its own accord through the materiality of listening experience, if the artistic process is repurposed towards cooperation. Composing sociality thus entails designing tools and sound art situations that, instead of steering the community towards a pre-defined outcome, would make new emergent socialities possible.

Similarly, composers and sound artists Perdro Rebelo and Rodrigo Cicchelli Velloso (2018) propose adopting sound art forms, such as field recordings, soundwalks and sound installations to socially engaged practice of participatory pedagogy, using their work in the Brazilian favelas as a case study. Exploring material and social mediations of sound affords the artists a particular method of community-building and a means of social inclusion. Rebelo and Velloso (2018, 152) conclude that "[s]ound represents a privileged medium for engaging in participatory work precisely because of the difficulties in articulating listening as an experience, its personal character", facilitating "an understanding of how [sound environments] too make up what we are, as individuals and communities".

That is not to say that no sound artists are critical of participation. Atau Tanaka and Adam Parkinson (2018) explicitly write of "the problems with participation" in their eponymous article. They explore the "ways in which participation-driven approaches can work, but also consider when they break downs and the pitfalls they engender", using their projects from the past decade as a starting point for this discussion (Tanaka and Parkinson 2018, 156). To Tanaka and Parkinson, the biggest concern is with how participation may become instrumentalised by the state or the market. However, they also find a resistance potential in sound and music practices as emphasising tacit—embodied and unarticulated—forms of knowledge over symbolic ones. Tacit sonic knowledges engender contingent forms of participation that escape the dominant discourses and thus become harder to co-opt.

5.4.2 Audiences

My ethnographic case studies of participant perspectives in sound art, while unquestionably too small to make generalised conclusions, remain, to my knowledge, the only ones of their kind. An expanded view of participatory soundmaking can be glimpsed, however, from contextualising my results against the studies of participation in music. In the following, I draw on two such studies: Thomas Turino's ethnomusicological account of traditional participatory music practices in his book *Music as Social Life: Politics of Participation* (2008) and the research project "CONNECT— the public as artists" at Max Planck Institute for Empirical Aesthetics that investigated audience participation in contemporary avantgarde music (Toelle and Sloboda 2021; Toelle 2022). While neither study explicitly employed Mead's perspective theory, their discussion of publics' practices and attitudes provide enough information to reconstruct the audience's perspectives.

Turino (2008, 26), as I mentioned in the introduction, counterposes participatory performance as one of the four principal forms of musicking with the Western modernity's entrenched understanding of music as concert music—"presentational performance" in his terms. The difference in the audience's relation to the musical material leads to a noticeable difference in experience. Concert music is primarily meant for listening. In participatory performance, however, listening takes a back seat, while the main component of the aesthetic experience is the feeling of community that musicking together brings. Although such performances may include non-soundmaking roles (e.g., dancers), Turino does not see them as less participatory or less contributing to the whole than soundmaking ones. However, he notes that individual virtuosity and self-expression are largely discouraged in participatory music practices, as they would take away from the social cohesion.

The categories that dominate Turino's (2008) account of participatory performances are repetition and stability. They manifest strongly on both sonic and social levels. Among the features common to most participatory music traditions he names such traits as constant rhythm and metre, repetitive open forms without clear beginning or end, dense monotonous textures and a pronounced lack of contrast or "extensive variation" (Turino 2008, 59). This repetitiveness applies also on a grander scale, in the relatively limited repertoire of musical pieces that can be performed in such settings. These aspects do not provide for a particularly exciting long-form listening; their goal is rather to maintain the accessibility of participation and create a state of social unity. However, on a more symbolic level, they also serve to reinforce the community's cultural identity and preserve its cultural memory. Participation in such practices is predicated on the participants' belonging to a given group and at the same time reinscribes the group identity onto their bodies through performance.

Already from this brief description, both points of connection and difference emerge between the public's perspective in traditional participatory music and sound art. On the one hand, much like in Turino's account, the participants in my case studies also emphasised sociality and community-building as crucial parts of their experiences. On the other hand, that lead to quite different sonic results.

While some of the features Turino describes—open forms, dense textures, some degree of repetitiveness—could be clearly heard in *Let Us Sing Your Place*, others were not. As discussed in detail, the performance largely relies on experimental and unusual vocal sounds and an exploratory ethos. The participants experienced a sense of community not because they were a stable group engaging in a familiar activity, but on the contrary because they were a collection of strangers doing something new together. Rather than reinforcing existing identities and beliefs, the performance challenged them.

In case of *Speaker Sculptures*, some of the activities I observed were, in fact, participatory performance practices in Turino's sense—such as community singing or karaoke. And the predominant way of interacting with the works—playing music recordings through them—did exhibit a certain degree of repetitiveness. However, those should not be interpreted as performances of existing cultural identities either: the choice of music to play or perform was not dictated by the participants' cultural backgrounds. Moreover, the interaction between the music chosen and the sculpture produced a dialectic of familiarity and novelty rather than just reinscribing familiarity. These activities can be seen as forms of referential identity-building characteristic of the digital condition (see Stalder 2017): creating something new and personalised from recombining existing materials.

A more experimental sound world and a firm rootedness in modern culture are also characteristic of contemporary music composition that was the subject of CONNECT project. At the same time, participation in this case was framed by concert music practices and institutions, making it distinctly different from both traditional participatory music and sound art.

The research revolved around two pieces by the composers Christian Mason and Huang Ruo that were commissioned by three European ensembles with the stipulation that they must include audience participation. Both composers chose to score the audience parts, although in Ruo's piece the instructions were more open-form and improvisational. For that reason, rather than invite spontaneous on-the-spot participation the way both traditional and sound art practices do, a number of workshops and rehearsals were organised for the participants to learn their parts—but also for the composers to adapt their pieces to the participants' abilities (Toelle and Sloboda 2021).

The conflicting goals of presentational and participatory music that became intertwined in this project largely resulted in the participants' perspectives being somewhat conflicted and contradictory. The CONNECT researchers Jutta Toelle and John Sloboda (2021) note, for example, that while the participants rated their enjoyment of the experience almost universally high, they did not have anything specific to say about the music itself. Instead, they concentrated on the social activity of participation. At the same time, respondents diverged greatly on its relationship to the listening experience: some found participation to be interfering with their listening, while others claimed that it helped them to really hear the music for the first time. Toelle and Sloboda (2021, 79) point out that while "most participants [were] regular attenders of classical and contemporary music concerts" and thus familiar with the respective sonic and listening practices, that also made it harder for them to diverge from the concertgoer perspective.

The institutional frame of concert music also imposed a sharper role differentiation than what Turino (2008) prescribes for participatory music. Composers, performers and participating audiences in the CONNECT project possessed distinctly different degrees of creative agency. Some of the participants even noted that the structure of the concert hall clearly separating the artists from the audiences negatively impacted their sense of community. Overall, the participants assessed their roles as performers and contributors, but not necessarily on equal footing with the musicians—and definitely not with the composers. They perceived "closeness to professionals; the feeling that they had been let in on professional secrets" (Toelle and Sloboda 2021, 80)—a formulation that maintains the divide between the two groups.

Participatory sound art, as it is framed by the modern institutions of art, is also characterised by a stronger role differentiation than traditional participatory music. My respondents similarly assessed their creative agencies as somewhat unequal to the artists. One of the participants in *Let Us Sing Your Place*, for example, described her role in the performance as "a co-creator, but a subordinate one", as Faber guided them through the process. However, as both my interviews and the statements in the previous subsection show, sound artists working with participation pointedly refrain from controlling the soundmaking activity of their audiences. They concentrate their creative agency in the act of invitation—of taking the perspective of a listener and instilling in the audience the perspective of a co-creator, either verbally or through the mediation of the work's materialities—not least of them sonic, engaging with the sound's ability to evoke a response.

This largely resolves the clash of agencies that Toelle and Sloboda observed in participatory music, leading the audience to feel freer to exercise their creativity within the frame of the artwork. It also resulted in a tighter interweaving of listening and participation, with most of my respondents claiming that both aspects were equally important to them and some even pointing to the impossibility of separating the two. In other words, in becoming co-creators, the participants remain listeners, the two perspectives fusing together and making the participants reassess their attitudes towards sonic phenomena and experiences.

This fusion of perspectives reveals participation in sound art to be a form of art *reception*, a way of experiencing sound—as something we *make* rather than something we are subjected to. Approaching the sonic experience that way unsettles a number of conventional ideas about sound. Participatory context reveals a possibility for the aesthetic appreciation of "ugly" and unusual sounds, often perceived as undesirable in presentational music performances. Dissociating soundmaking from music, participatory sound art liberates its audiences from the culturally entrenched protocols of aesthetic judgement, revealing its underlying ableism and exclusivism. It furthermore facilitates empathy and openness, manifesting in the altruistic performativity of *Let Us Sing Your Place* or in the chance social encounters that *Speaker Sculptures* encourage (see Keylin 2020). In that manner, participatory sound art further questions the connection between voice and subjectivity—both through the explorations of the constructed and mediated character of literal and metaphorical vocality and through offering horizontal and altruistic ways of exercising creativity, beyond the egocentrism of self-expression.

References

Bala, Sruti. 2018. *The gestures of participatory art*. Manchester: Manchester University Press.

Barthes, Roland. 1977. The grain of the voice. In *Image, music, text*. Translated by Stephen Heath, 179–189. New York: Hill and Wang.
Baschet, François, and Bernard Baschet. 1987. Sound sculpture: Sounds, shapes, public participation, education. *Leonardo* 20: 107–114.
Beuys, Joseph. 1974. I am searching for field character. In *Art into society, society into art: Seven German artists*, ed. Caroline Tisdall, 48. London: Institute of Contemporary Art.
Bishop, Claire. 2012. *Artificial hells: Participatory art and the politics of spectatorship*. London: Verso Books.
Cage, John. 1961. *Silence: Lectures and writings*. Middletown, CT: Wesleyan University Press.
Eco, Umberto. 1989. *The open work*. Translated by Anna Cancogni. Cambridge, MA: Harvard University Press.
Faber, Katrine. 2019. Singing our place. *Performance Research* 24: 7–16. https://doi.org/10.1080/13528165.2019.1593730.
Felski, Rita. 2017. How is an art work an agent? *Academic Quarter* 16: 163–169.
Glaveanu, Vlad Petre. 2013. Rewriting the language of creativity: The five A's framework. *Review of General Psychology* 17: 69–81. https://doi.org/10.1037/a0029528.
———. 2015. Creativity as a sociocultural act. *The Journal of Creative Behavior* 49: 165–180.
Groth, S.K., and K. Samson. 2017. Sound art situations. *Organised Sound* 22: 101–111. https://doi.org/10.1017/S1355771816000388.
Kester, Grant. 2011. *The one and the many: Contemporary collaborative art in a global context*. Durham, NC: Duke University Press.
Keylin, Vadim. 2020. Postcritical listening: Political affordances in participatory sound art. *Organised Sound* 25: 353–361.
Kim-Cohen, Seth. 2009. *In the blink of an ear: Toward a non-cochlear sonic art*. New York and London: Continuum.
Lanza, Joseph. 2016. *Elevator music: A surreal history of Muzak, easy-listening and other moodsong*. Ann Arbor: University of Michigan Press.
Latour, Bruno. 1994. On technical mediation. *Common Knowledge* 3: 29–64.
Licht, Alan. 2019. *Sound art revisited*. New York and London: Bloomsbury.
Neuhaus, Max. 1994. The broadcast works and Audium. In *Zeitgleich: The symposium, the seminar, the exhibition*. Vienna: Triton.
Rebelo, Pedro, and Rodrigo Cicchelli Velloso. 2018. Participatory sonic arts: The Som de Maré project—Towards a socially engaged art of sound in the everyday. In *The Routledge research companion to electronic music—reaching out with technology*, ed. Simon Emmerson, 137–155. Abingdon: Routledge.
Schafer, R. Murray. 1993. *The soundscape: Our sonic environment and the tuning of the world*. New York: Simon and Schuster.
Stalder, Felix. 2017. *The digital condition*. Hoboken, NJ: Wiley-Blackwell.

Tanaka, Atau, and Adam Parkinson. 2018. The problems with participation. In *Routledge companion to electronic music: Reaching out with technology*, ed. Simon Emmerson, 156–177. Routledge.

Taruskin, Richard. 2010. *Music in the late twentieth century*. Oxford: Oxford University Press.

Toelle, Jutta. 2022. Just join in? Audience participation in classical contemporary music: Empirical insights into theory and practice. In *Tuning up! The innovative potential of Musikvermittlung*, 199–214. Bielefeld: transcript.

Toelle, Jutta, and John A. Sloboda. 2021. The audience as artist? The audience's experience of participatory music. *Musicae Scientiae* 25: 67–91. https://doi.org/10.1177/1029864919844804.

Tonelli, Chris. 2016. Ableism and the reception of improvised soundsinging. *Music and Politics* 10: 1–14. https://doi.org/10.3998/mp.9460447.0010.204.

Turino, Thomas. 2008. *Music as social life: The politics of participation*. Chicago: University of Chicago Press.

Weidman, Amanda. 2015. Voice. In *Keywords in sound*, ed. David Novak and Matt Sakakeeny, 232–246. Durham, NC: Duke University Press.

White, Gareth. 2013. *Audience participation in theatre: Aesthetics of the invitation*. New York: Palgrave Macmillan.

Woodruff, Jeremy. 2020. Composing sociality: Toward an aesthetics of transition design. In *The Bloomsbury handbook of sound art*, ed. Sanne Krogh Groth and Holger Schulze, 41–88. New York, London: Bloomsbury.

CHAPTER 6

Gestures

Abstract This chapter approaches the politics of participation in sound art from a postcritical perspective. It employs Sruti Bala's theory of gesture—an action that is at the same time inherently aesthetic and socially and politically embedded—to discuss the political potentialities of sound artworks, while not limiting them to critical statements or explicitly activist projects. The chapter examines the political gestures of participatory sound art at two levels: the artworks themselves as gestures expressing a political sentiment and a political pragmatics, and the gestures of the participants performed in the context of sound artworks. It identifies three fundamental areas of participatory sound art's politics: concern, empowerment and togetherness. Rather than laying bare "matters of fact" and forgone conclusions, gestures of concern engage the participants viscerally by putting them in the first-person perspective of performing the critical interpretation. At the same time, gestures of empowerment and togetherness rely on sound's ability to operate across both physical and social barriers and create a sense of community while sustaining difference. The politics of participatory sound art can thus be described as "politics of the possible"—of enabling political imaginaries, both utopian and dystopian.

Keywords Politics of sound • Postcritique • Matters of concern • Empowerment • Antagonism • Political possibility

6.1 Sonic Gestures Between Symbols and Actions

The complex entanglement of the artists' and audiences' creative agencies and perspectives explored in the previous chapter has further implications for the politics of participatory sound art. Contrary to the often-raised accusations in political apathy, sounds artists do indeed envisage their works in explicitly political terms, even when not necessarily pursuing explicitly political goals. However, the contingent and emergent character of sonic participation, its being composed of a multitude of individual undirected actions—creative and receptive, purposeful and accidental, human and non-human—makes the straightforward models of critical or activist art hardly applicable.

At the same time, the shifts in audiences' perspectives effected by the experience of collective soundmaking mean that the entrenched avant-garde *modus operandi* of "didactical provocation" (Kester 2011, 9) simply no longer works. In the context of participatory sound art, the typically provocative sonic content—unusual and unmusical sounds—fails to provoke, instead being readily embraced by the audiences as a means of fostering horizontality and communality. Nor is didacticism part of the sound art's ethos—neither aesthetic, as evidenced by the Baschet quote in previous chapter, nor political, as, for example, Christina Kubisch notes:

> I have always been critical toward the way that people deal with technology and have made many pieces about the relationships between nature and technology. But I never point a finger and say, "This is bad" or "This is good." I'm more interested in having people recognize what's around them by doing it themselves. I could tell everyone that I think it's bad. But that wouldn't be an *experience*. (Cox and Kubisch 2006)

Even in extreme cases, such as Ultra-Red's "militant sound investigations", sound art tends to approach the political with an openness rooted in the figure of listening, rejecting the possibility of a priori knowledge and condemning the kind of "activism [that] undertakes research for the purpose of composing fixed analyses that then drive participation" and "presumes an object/subject division: those who act as ideological patrons and those in need of patronage" (Ultra-red 2008, 6).

A more implicit kind of non-didactical politics—or politics as experience—emerged in my observations of *Speaker Sculptures* and *Let Us Sing Your Place* as well. Both artists expressed political sensibilities that informed their work without imposing it on the participants. Katrine Faber directly invoked ecological themes, while Benoît Maubrey referred to the general avantgarde tradition of playful disobedience, wishing for his sculptures to facilitate "a small revolution in the street". Both works also exhibited the power to foster connections and emergent communities. In *Lest Us Sing Your Place*, the participants assumed an altruistic ethos, wilfully subduing the ego in favour of creating something together. In case of *Speakers' Arena*, installed in one of Berlin's immigrant quarters, bordering the gay village, I observed many spontaneous friendly social encounters between strangers.

My contention, detailed in Chap. 3, is that the political sensibility characteristic of participatory sound art is distinctly postcritical and its workings are best addressed through the concept of the gesture. Discussing the emergent collectivities enacted by lyric poetry—both in the process of live performance and in transhistorical and transcultural exchange—Francesco Giusti (2019, 2021) draws on Agamben's (1993, 1999) notion of the gesture as a mechanism of this enactment. To Giusti, a gesture is an action cut off from its causality and teleology, which gives it the power to interrupt—but also to be infinitely re-enacted. Thus,

[A]n idea of gestural communities can be envisioned: communities based on the shareability of gestures, not on reciprocal identification among individuated subjects nor on communal knowledge nor on identical responses to literary works. [...] These gestures are not primarily offered as meaningful actions directed to a specific goal; they come before any acquisition of contextual meaning and socio-historical purpose. (Giusti 2021, 99, 102)

This conception of the gesture evokes Tia DeNora's explanation of meaning-making in music through the notion of affordance:

[T]he concept of "affordance" captures music's role as ... a "mediator" of the social. And depending upon how it is conceptualised, the concept of "affordance" highlights music's potential as an organising medium, as something that helps to structure such things as styles of consciousness, ideas, or modes of embodiment. To speak of music as affording things is to suggest that it is a material against which things are shaped up, elaborated through practical and sometimes non-conscious action. (DeNora 2003, 46–47)

While in a traditional concert music situation the structures in question are given, in participatory sound art they emerge from the participants' interactions and gestures. As an action abstracted from its teleology and the context of its production, gesture occupies a space in-between an act (in Heinrich's [2014] sense) and a form (in Levine's [2015] sense). It affords a similar mechanism of shaping meanings and socialities against itself, both for its maker and for the others, collectively. It can thus offer a mechanism through which perspective-taking may place in a shared soundmaking experience without—and perhaps more efficiently than—a direct discursive exchange.

The in-betweenness of gesture and its importance for the politics of participation is emphasised by Sruti Bala (2018). While not a political act with a measurable impact, a gesture embeds the political in the aesthetic and vice versa by both manifesting a form and referring to a social function. Bala further points to Carries Noland's (2010) reading of the gesture as a site of resistance where the entrenched techniques of the body, performatively maintaining the status quo, are met with individual creative and political agency. Similarly, in his book *Gestures of Concern*, Chris Ingraham (2020, 2) examines the "noninstrumental expressive acts" ranging from attending a protest to posting a photo online that are performed out of concern for the state of public affairs. While "their measurable impact remains imperceptible", they are "affectively generative", enacting empowerment and helping political change take hold (Ingraham 2020, 2–3). Furthermore, the gestures of concern facilitate the emergence of an "affective commonwealth"—"a shared attunement and response-ability to one another" (Ingraham 2020, 131). As I will discuss in the sections below, concern, empowerment and togetherness are closely entangled in the gestures of participatory sound art as well.

Among the dichotomies that the gesture suspends is also the artist-audience divide. On the one hand, the artworks themselves can be approached as gestures expressing a political sentiment and a political pragmatics. On the other hand, the gestures of the participants can also be infused with political meaning, co-creating not just the aesthetics, but also the politics of sound artworks. Bala (2018, 80) explores this suspension through her category of "unsolicited gestures" that I briefly discussed in Chap. 3—participants actions that go "beyond the roles and options offered to them". She proposes that participation in art operates two dimensions: one organised, offered by the artists, the other unsolicited—breaking with the contract of participation expressed in the artist's invitation. Moreover, this dimension is crucial in the unfolding of the participatory art's politics, as it represents the non-scripted agency of the participants.

Examples of unsolicited gestures abound in most empirical accounts of participatory sound art. In "Sound art/Street life", Cristabel Stirling (2016) examines the negative reactions to sound artworks in public space. Among her case studies, she narrates the controversy around Catalina Pollak's interactive installation *Phantom Railings* (2013). Installed at the fence of the Mall Street Garden in London, the work, when hit by a passer-by's shadow, would produce the sound of hitting a metallic railing. One night, *Phantom Railings* were vandalised by the homeless people who slept in the garden and with whose sleep the work of the work interfered. This act of silencing the sound can be read as an unsolicited gesture of sonic participation, revealing, as Stirling argues, the antagonistic claims to the public space.

Unsolicited gestures, however, are not necessarily antagonistic. They can be "at times defiant, at times cooperative, and at times evasive. [...] The examples of unsolicited participation could lay bare an antagonistic or oppositional dimension, but they could also serve to reassert the status quo" (Bala 2018, 81, 91). One can also add that they can be reparative and activist. Atau Tanaka and Adam Parkinson (2018, 169), for example, recount how one of their participatory sound workshops that was "meant to be about gaming was appropriated by our participants to create an interactive tool to present education pathways".

Tanaka and Parkinson's example shows how the notion of unsolicited participation opens up the political possibility of ostensibly apolitical works as, in a sense, any participant gesture of political expression would be unsolicited in their context. In the following sections, however, I want to focus on participatory sound art that engages the political themes more or less directly. While by no means exhaustive, the examples below offer an insight into how participatory sound art balances politics and experientiality, performing concern and empowerment in place of critique and didacticism.

6.2 Gestures of Concern

Discussing ecological sound art in her article "The Sonic Aftermath", Anette Vandsø (2020, 23) ponders the "epistemological potential" of artworks that present unedited field recordings or straightforward data sonifications of ecological processes. "[N]ot merely referring to an already gained scientific knowledge", she argues, sound artworks "redistribute what can and cannot be heard and what can and cannot be recognized as significant sounds or even a voice in a political debate" (Vandsø 2020, 30, 32). Facilitating affective engagement by staging "the scientific matter of fact" in the listeners' lifeworlds, they transform it into "a matter of concern" (Vandsø 2020, 39).

Ecological sensibilities are not alien to participatory sound art either. In 2020, Kaffe Matthews launched a variation of the sonic bike called the *Enviro Bike*. Instead of matching the rider's GPS coordinates to a pre-programmed sound map, the new bike was equipped with a pollution sensor installed on its handlebars and sonified its data in real time. The four bikes presented at the project's launch at the *Lisboa Soa* festival all used different sample banks, ranging from "thunderous rackets of parping fog horns" to "cyber woman calmly presenting the effects of invisible molecules on the human animal" (Matthews 2020, n.p.).

Like other sonic bikes, the *Enviro Bike* belongs to the category of augmented sound art, making audible the phenomena already present in the environment but hidden from the human senses. In this regard, it operates similarly to the artworks that Vandsø discusses: by transforming the dry scientific data that only fine measurement devices can register (matter of fact) into a sensory experience (matter of concern). What I want to explore here is how interactivity and participation help enact this concern.

As is the case with many augmented sound artworks, *Enviro Bike* has a ludic quality—a scavenger hunt for hidden sounds, even though these sounds represent real danger. Matthews (2020, n.p.) notes that riders in Lisbon "wanted to explore their local neighbourhood and discover how polluted or not their local streets were, and where and when do the peaks arise". Participatory sound art thus becomes a form of Socratic pedagogy: rather than explicitly confronting the participants with an ecological issue, it allows them to discover the issue on their own through exploration of their environment. Unlike most of the works discussed by Vandsø, it engages with concern indirectly, through fostering curiosity and exploration.

Furthermore, participation places the listener at the centre of the action. It makes them internalise the concern by assuming a first-person position. In other words, participatory sound art turns concern into a performative gesture that the participants re-enact. And as perspectives, according to Mead (1972 [1934]) and his followers (e.g., Martin 2005; Glaveanu 2018), stem from an intention to act in certain way, performing this gesture makes the participants assume a perspective of ecological concern.

The *Enviro Bike* does not just immerse the listener into a sonified pollution-scape of their city. It makes them perform concern for it by actively investigating and measuring the concentrations of particulate matter. That it is done by way of biking adds a further layer to the message, as it moves the participants to reflect on different modes of transportation and their ecological impact.

A similar shift from purely intellectual to intellectual-affective engagement—from critique to concern—can be observed in participatory sound art that deals with social topics. In 2015, Matthews created a sonic bike ride *Finding Song Home* in Brussels. The work took the rider along the streets of the EU's capital followed by stories and songs of the legal and illegal immigrants living in the city that Matthews collected while doing an artistic residency. Counterpointing the geography of the prosperous centre of the pan-European project with the itineraries of those excluded from it, the work has the rider perform concern for "the injustices of birthright and questions the powers that enable or prevent the free movement of citizens" (Matthews 2015, n.p.).

For a typical rider—likely white, European and middle-class—the work may very well be provocative and antagonistic, making them face the exclusivity of the Western freedom taken for granted by those who enjoy it. As the bike's loudspeakers broadcast the work's sonic content onto the public space, the participant transmits the artist's gesture of concern further—to the people they ride by. The rider thus not only experiences the provocation and antagonism themselves, but also serves as a vehicle of provocation for the secondary audience.

However, rather than constructing the immigrant as the Other with whose existence the listener has to be confronted, *Finding Song Home* has the riders assume the immigrant perspective in the first person. Participation here operates somewhat akin to lyric subjectivity in poetry: by having the reader (the participants) inhabit the lyric "I" (the voices) of the work, taking on their experiences and narratives.[1] Thus, the work does not only disturb and discomfort the participants, but also fosters empathy and

---

[1] On lyric subjectivity, see for example (Culler 2015, Chap. 3).

compassion—it simultaneously challenges the perspective of the rider and has them take the perspective of the Other.

That is, of course, when it is indeed the Other. Operating in the public space rather than in the white cube of the gallery, *Finding Song Home* invites participation also from those unlikely to attend the gallery. For a rider with an immigrant background, enacting the same gesture of concern would provide a vastly different experience—one of solidarity and affirmation rather than provocation and antagonism.

Concern thus reveals itself to be a broader category than critique—one that includes both antagonism and compassion. The empathy-building potential of participation has been commented upon by the artists and theorists of participation already in the 1990s. As I mentioned in Chap. 2, Suzi Gablik (1995) directly connects empathy and compassion to listening—as opposed to the lack of affect found in vision. It is hardly surprising that empathy often complements—if not outright overrides—critique in sound art, which, as Alan Licht (2019, 6) argues "is conceived in terms of listener-to-listener relationship between the artist and the audient".

The position of a listener, furthermore, is necessarily relational and socially and ecologically co-constructed. According to Salomé Voegelin (2010, xii), "the listener [is] intersubjectively constituted in perception, while producing the very thing he perceives". Jean-Luc Nancy (2007, 21–22) speaks even more radically of "the subject of the listening or the subject who is listening (but also the one who is 'subject to listening' in the sense that one can be 'subject to' unease, an ailment, or a crisis)" that is "perhaps no subject at all, except as the place of resonance" for the sounding agencies of the human and non-human Others.

A gesture of sharing a listening perspective then can be understood as a gesture of sharing a concern. In the context of participatory sound art, however, the listening is not just communicated, but re-enacted. Performing it from the perspective of the Other produces a gesture of concern even when the listening itself is not explicitly activist—and can in fact be introspective and intimate.

Perhaps the most prominent example of a participatory listening practice in sound art are Pauline Oliveros' *Sonic Meditations* as they informed much of the later sonic thinking. The cornerstone of Oliveros' music philosophy and practice of Deep Listening, *Meditations* are text scores, often using poetic or evocative language, that can be performed by both professional musicians and laypersons, solo or in groups. The scores do not necessarily produce performances for secondary audiences—some of the pieces do not produce any audible sounds at all but rather instruct the performer to listen in a certain way. Sharon Stewart (2020, 224) argues that they "hack" the Western art music idea of a score "as a vehicle to transfer a sonic construct that could be measured or externally analyzed" making it instead "a vehicle for exploring more internal and intersocial questions, the unfathomable workings of perception and consciousness".

As the title suggests, *Meditations* are fundamentally an introspective practice aimed at achieving the state of radical attentiveness "to the whole space/time continuum of sound/silences" (Oliveros 2005, xxv). They were furthermore composed in the 1960s and 1970s against a historical background defined by violence and social unrest. It would be easy then to read the pieces as escapist, avoiding the engagement with the political reality by turning one's attention inwards.

However, this would be a misinterpretation. As Stewart (2020) points out, Oliveros practiced *Sonic Meditations* and Deep Listening concurrently with her queer feminist activism, suggesting a deep connection between the two. At the same time, the radical attentiveness that *Meditations* foster includes the attentiveness towards the social and the cultural rather than bracketing it off. Political issues, Steward (2020, 257) argues, "are not just to be pointed out, discussed or problematized, but they can also be engaged with—through listening, through sound making, through music making" which creates "new models for being together in the sonic commons". An introspective gesture of hyper-aware listening can thus itself become a gesture of concern.

6.3 Gestures of Empowerment

In an interview with Martha Mockus, Oliveros says of her Deep Listening practice:

> [I]t's very important to me to help facilitate creative process in others, to empower people to understand and use sound as a force in their lives and in their realization of who they are, creatively and spiritually. And in this way, you build community. You build a community of understanding based on sounding and listening. (Oliveros in Mockus 2007, 164)

The idea of empowerment is one of the cornerstones of the participatory art discourse. As such, it has been the subject of much critique, pointing to its nebulousness and even possibly hollowness. On the one hand, the questions of power remain: who gets empowered and who decides who gets empowered (Tanaka and Parkinson 2018). On the other hand, empowerment within a clearly defined institutional frame of art does not necessarily transcend into the realm of the everyday suffused by powerlessness (see, e.g., Bishop 2006a; Bala 2018).

While acknowledging these critiques, it is important not to dismiss the experiences of the participants, who often *do* profess a sense of empowerment. For example, in 2019 I talked with some of the riders participating in Kaffe Matthews' bike opera *Ispod Fontana* in Zagreb. They told me that riding a sonic bike with sounds blasting from it made them feel empowered to lay their claim to the public space of the city that is severely lacking the infrastructure and culture of biking.

The kind of empowerment that both Oliveros and the participants in *Ispod Fontana* talk about can be understood as a gesture. Even if "artistic models of democracy have only a tenuous relationship to actual forms of democracy" (Bishop 2006b, 10), judging art in terms of quantifiable impact, as Bala (2018) argues, misses the point, burdening the artists with the task of NGOs. Rather, empowerment attained in participation can be performative—an aesthetic gesture without an immediate teleology that can nevertheless become internalised and be drawn upon outside of the art frame (Ingraham 2020).

In 2022, the artists Amanda Gutiérrez and Veronica Mockler launched the project *Sono-soro[walks]* consisting of an online soundwalking score, a database of audio records sent in response to the score and an augmented reality soundwalk based on these recordings. The project focuses on the experience of walking at night of "female-identifying, two-spirit, non-binary and trans individuals". Gutiérrez and Mockler write:

> This score is meant to be performed at night, but we are aware of the dangers that walking at night represents for many identities and bodies. It is precisely the RIGHT TO WALK AT NIGHT that our project aims to help reclaim. Therefore, we invite you to please record yourself in public space at night only when you feel safe doing so with your collaborators and allies. We invite you listen with care to your own collective capacities and personal limits while in urban space. (Gutiérrez and Mockler 2022, n.p.; capitalisation in the original)

The score asks the participants to perform and record three sonic gestures: a verbal response to a public address on the gender violence, a sound or sounds made with their own body and their material environment and a soundscape of their walk. Each of these gestures can be read as one of both concern and empowerment: listening to a soundscape of a night walk juxtaposes the hyper-attentiveness of navigating an unsafe environment with the hyper-attentiveness of a sonic meditation and the sense of connection and community that it brings. Soundmaking focuses on one's body as an object of oppression, but at the same time as a source of agency to resist the oppression. Making a sound during a night walk means drawing attention to oneself, defying the imposed conducts of "safe" behaviour. Finally, lending one's voice—both physically and metaphorically—to continuing the polylogue on gender violence builds a sense of solidarity between the oppressed. Gutiérrez and Mockler refer here to Marcela Lagarde's (2006) notion of *sororidad*, or sisterhood—"women's mutual recognition and unity in public action, a kind of meeting point among women, through which they can build an alternative together" (Alonso 2005, n.p.). These gestures rely on the act of recording to sound out both "collective capacities and personal limits" brought about by the systems of oppression (Gutiérrez and Mockler 2022, n.p.).

At the same time, soundwalking itself can constitute a gesture. According to Andrea Polli (2017, 82), "the practice of soundwalking allows for an active engagement with the soundscape, but the practice could also be seen as closely tied to political actions. As if engaged in a political demonstration, soundwalkers can move through space in a silent protest." While not a protest action per se, *Sono-soro[walks]* invite the participants to act in defiance of their systemic oppression, finding empowerment in their shared sonic experiences. The project does not possess the power to make walking at night safe for its participants. However, it affords them, through a hyper-attentive listening that integrates the discursive with the experiential, a sense of individual and collective political agency that is creatively articulated in their recordings.

From the recordings they collected, Gutiérrez and Mockler designed an augmented reality soundwalk in central Berlin, mapping them along the footpath that ran through some backyards along the bank of the Spree. The walk was first performed in May 2022 but remains available via a soundwalking app *Echoes*.[2] The artists wove together voices and walks of women recorded in various parts of New York and Montreal with the recordings of March 8 women's protests in Istanbul and a reading of Elena Biserna's walking manifesto, creating a powerful dialectics of oppression and resistance, concern and empowerment. But in some sense, the most empowering feature of *Sono-soro[walks]* are the sounds of footsteps caught in the audio recordings, particularly in the last part of the walk that is a recording of a group soundwalk. Listening to the others' footsteps and others' voices creates the impression that the listener is not walking alone, emboldening them to venture forth on their night walk supported by the feeling of solidarity and strength in numbers.

Performing sonic gestures of empowerment in an art setting can be seen as therapeutic as it teaches the participants "to understand and use sound as a force in their lives" (Oliveros in Mockus 2007, 164). It is little wonder that participatory sound artworks, with their emphasis on immediate accessibility and dialogical, horizontal interactions, can sometimes explicitly be used in music therapy. Beginning in the 1970s, the Baschet brothers almost completely repurposed their sound sculptures from art exhibitions to therapeutic and educational projects. For example, from 1975 to 1978 they participated in the Guggenheim Museum program *Learning to Read through Arts*, which at that time was aimed at children who did not have access to regular schooling. In the 1980s and 1990s they collaborated with autism and disability organisations *MESH— Musique dans l'Éducation et le Soin des Handicapés* (Music in Education and Care of the Disabled Persons) and *Association Koschise*, developing therapeutic sound sculptures that would help autistic children acquire communication skills.

The Baschets' works mentioned above can generally be described as forms of community music therapy, which explicitly "addresses mechanisms of exclusion and inclusion" as a socially and politically engaged therapeutic practice (Trondalen and Bonde 2012, 51). That sound art can become an efficient medium of such interventions stems from its affordances that emphasise openness, experimentation and connectivity. For example, many of the Baschets' educational sculptures were designed to be played by a child and an adult simultaneously, "establishing a non-verbal dialog" (Baschet and Baschet 1987, 112). At the same time, they

---

[2] As I was not able to participate in the May event, my analysis is based on the experience of walking *Sono-soro[walks]* on my own with the help of the app in October 2022.

did not resemble traditional instruments, and therefore did not instil anxiety, an expectation of a "good" result in the player. The sculptures were built around a palette of timbres rather than traditional pitch scales to encourage the participants to experiment and learn without the fear of lacking skills.

The idea of empowerment has a strong sonic component to it expressed in the metaphor of "having a voice" and letting it be heard (Weidman 2015). With her sound installation *Ayumee-aawach-Oomama-mowan: Speaking to Their Mother* (1991), the Anishinaabe Canadian artist Rebecca Belmore amplified the voices of an oppressed community in a literal sense. The work originated from the dispute between the government of the Canadian town of Oka and the local Mohawk community: the town made plans for a golf course on the native burial lands that the Mohawk considered sacred. Belmore installed a giant megaphone at the contested site for the community to speak directly to the land as "protests often fall upon deaf government ears" (Belmore in Lippard 1997, 15).

In Hannah Arendt's (1958, 22–78) concept of the political, any political action is necessarily public—and vice versa, any public action is necessarily political. While for Arendt her approach to political was necessary to extend it beyond institutionalised politics, her insistence on the publicity made it exclusory as well. Judith Butler (2016, 20) in "Rethinking Vulnerability and Resistance" notes that "all public assembly is haunted by the police and the prison. And every public square is defined in part by the population that could not possibly arrive there." Even those able to appear in the public space physically may still be excluded from the public discourse. The public space is designated as such by the structures of power, who strive to maintain a control over it. By moving the site of political expression from the colonialist city to the indigenous sacred grounds, Belmore's installation questions what space is considered public and who gets to define it. As Gascia Ouzounian argues:

> *Ayumee-aawach Oomama-mowan: Speaking to Their Mother* shifts the location of a public forum from the centres of power to remote areas, and as such reclaims the political worth of marginal (and marginalised) places. The installation draws attention to the uneven modes of exchange that determine who speaks, who listens and where; it shows that the place of political exchange is integral to that exchange, that the positions of political actors cannot be divorced from the 'place(s) from which they speak'. (Ouzounian 2013, 88)

6.4 Gestures of Togetherness

Belmore's installation, as well as *Sono-soro[walks]* and the Baschets' educational projects, make the point of engaging the participation of specific underprivileged groups or communities. This makes sense as this approach addresses the question of access to participation. I want to make a case here, however, for the possibility of the gestures of empowerment in participatory sound artworks that open themselves up to undefined audiences.

In her article "Silences and policies in the shared listening", Susana Jiménez Carmona (2020) discusses the question "who participates?" through a comparative analysis of two sound art groups: the American collective Ultra-Red and the Mexican Escuchatorio. Carmona notes the antithetical strategies of the two groups: while Ultra-Red produce their works through long collaborative process with specific communities, Escuchatorio operate through open calls for sound recordings on a certain theme posted on social media. The recordings sent in response to these calls are then broadcasted unedited in their entirety on a variety of online and offline radio stations. Four broadcasts have been produced between 2015 and 2017, the first responding with the recordings of protests to the anniversary of the Iguala kidnapping, where 43 students disappeared, allegedly abducted by the police in collusion with drug cartels. The following project explored somewhat more abstract, though still political, themes, such as silence or walking as acts of resistance.

According to Pedro Rebelo and Rodrigo Cicchelli Velloso (2018, 142), the practice of sound recording is "both familiar and foreign". Even though mobile recording technologies have become ubiquitous in contemporary culture, for the most part that concerns video rather than audio. Sound recording thus has the capacity to defamiliarise everyday experience (or one's self in case of recording one's voice), while remaining accessible and intuitive. Moreover, "what matters even more is what motivates one to record something in the first place. The action is inevitably embedded with meaning—perhaps a memory or a story fragment, a recognition of place" (Rebelo and Velloso 2018, 141).

Escuchatorio approaches sound recording "as a straightforward way of activating listening: if you stop to record something, you listen" (Carmona 2020, 120). In other words, it is a gesture that reshapes the recordist's perspective. Listening, following Voegelin (2010) and Nancy (2007), produces a relational subject, necessarily co-constituted by its social and material situatedness. A politically motivated listening, such as one prompted by the Escuchatorio calls (or, for that matter, the *Sono-soro[walks]* scores), articulated in a recording then produces a political subject, embedded both in a local community and in a global network of participation.

Addressing the critique of participatory art as promoting social cohesion at the cost of erasing otherness, Stirling (2016, n.p.) argues that "collaboration need not be about conversion, overcoming conflict, or flattening difference. […] Practices that are inclusive, sociable, and participatory can be progressive too—*if* they continue to acknowledge difference." In most cases, that means offering participation to specific communities the way Ultra-Red or the Baschets did it. However, Carmona (2020, 127) points that difference can also manifest in practices addressed to unspecified "*anyones*"—as diversity that emerges from connecting "far-away and diverse places where the voices which protest against a ubiquitous, multiform and deaf Power come from and arrive". Moreover, the empowerment and sociality produced through such global gestures can be passed on—beyond the spacetime of the artwork and within the local communities:

> This finding and listening to each other, albeit among a vague *us*, can help to sharpen the listening among the closer voices which are perhaps being silenced as well as to stop feeling alone, thus gathering strength for each one of the particular and diverse battles being fought. (Carmona 2020)

Escuchatorio's calls evoke Dewey's (1930 [1916]) idea of the public as emergent, arising in response to a problem or a shared interest. The participants—*anyones*—perform their concern for the issues suggested by the artists through applying it to their listening and audio recording practices. In the process, they emerge as a distributed community—"a vague *us* around the world" (Carmona 2020, 124)—of shared concern. As Escuchatorio broadcasts the participants' recordings they have collected, the community of concern expands to include the listeners of the broadcast, affectively engaging with the recordings and their subject matter. In this way, sound art's affordance for connectivity discussed in Chap. 4 manifests a political dimension through the participants' gestures that signal and invite togetherness.

Moreover, as the examples of Oliveros and Gutiérrez show, contrary to Alan Licht's (2019) claim that sound art's focus on listening leads to the loss of the social aspect of music, togetherness and a sense of community may emerge in listening itself. Indian sound artist and researcher Budhaditya Chattopadhyay (2023) proposes to expand the notion of "co-listening" beyond the narrow context of music and related online and offline social practices such as concert-going or sharing a musical stream. Instead, the term could mean "a socially and community-driven listening mode, in which listening together both in situ and online, reaches a whole new affective dimension of social cohesion nurturing solidarity" (Chattopadhyay 2023, 173). Co-listening forms an integral part of Chattopadhyay's creative methodology. In a number of "listening-driven workshop[s]" that the artist conducted at various geographical and institutional settings, he asked the participants to listen to the urban environment in order to find sites and sounds that "trigger a multitude of associative thoughts, imaginations, and/or personal memories" (Chattopadhyay 2023, 163) that were then shared among the group. This process aimed to "help [the participants] recognise the potential of listening to others in our environment not as bodies of conflict, but extension of the self as a larger common" (Chattopadhyay 2023, 162–163).

Togetherness is, of course, well-trodden ground of participatory art. The emergence of community in response to an artwork—and in particular sound art, as the example or *Turkish Jokes* shows—is the cornerstone of Bourriaud's (2002 [1998]) relational aesthetics. Much of relational art has been rightfully critiqued for addressing this community-raising call exclusively to gallery goers, thus perpetuating rather than transcending the social hierarchies. *Turkish Jokes*, however, was a public art piece and Escuchatorio distributed their calls on the internet, employing the connectivity of the internet to go beyond the art-institutional borders, and established initiatives such as mobile listening points to help the participants overcome the technological barriers. The audience of such gestures of togetherness is still limited geographically, linguistically or technologically (in case of *Turkish Jokes*, by design), but at the very minimum they operate across the entrenched class hierarchies.

Furthermore, the affordance for connectivity implies that community-raising gestures do not necessarily have to be initiated by the artists. Some of the participants in *Speakers' Arena* that I interviewed readily acknowledged that the sculpture had inspired them to interact with strangers. In some cases, the gesture was performed through the artwork itself—when, for example, a participant called the sculpture to address other people present on the square directly. In others, the participants' one-on-one interactions with the sculpture—playing their music, singing or performing—prompted others to talk to them. Many of these interactions occurred across class or ethnic borders, reflecting the unique character of the

Arena's site, situated at the meeting point of an immigrant quarter, Berlin's gay village, a gentrified area and a red lights district. At the same time, the sculpture also served as a way for the already existing local community to articulate itself in a number of impromptu concerts and other interactions.

In "Sound art/street life", Stirling (2016) contests the claims of urban sound theorists that public sound art fosters social engagement and community-building. Analysing the negative reactions—protests even—to Esther Ainsworth's installation *Bridge Links* (2013), she interprets them as evidence for Mouffe's (2013) theory of antagonism, as the artwork laid bare the claims of different groups to public space. The situation, however, may also be read from Deweian perspective: a community has emerged through their shared (even if possibly misguided) interest in preserving the local soundscape and ridding it of the intruding artwork. At the same time, Stirling (2016, n.p.) notes the emergence of a second community as well—of "young arty individuals [who] excitedly stopped in their tracks, eager to talk to invigilators". The conflict around *Bridge Links* thus illustrates Ryder's (2020) point that Dewey's and Mouffe's perspectives on democracy are not incompatible: community-building and antagonism emerged in this case as different aspects of the same process.

6.5 Sounds of the Possible

Performing concern, empowerment and togetherness, the gestures of participatory sound art reveal a different political modality from much of contemporary—visual or post-media—art. In *The Political Possibility of Sound*, Salomé Voegelin proposes to designate this modality as that of the possible. She cites the anthropologist Petra Rethmann (2013, 228), who coined the concept of the political possibility as an alternative to the "'politics of the antis': that is, a politics that can only imagine itself in terms of antagonism and opposition [...] and not in terms of building, invention, and creation". Rather, the politics of the possible unfolds in "the awkward and unstable engagement of dissimilarly situated subjects—authors and works—across difference" (Rethmann 2013, 237).

Difference is furthermore the cornerstone of Vlad Glaveanu's (2020) theory of the possible—a category he further connects to creativity. Both creativity in a narrow artistic sense and the creation of the possible in the broad sociocultural sense necessitate holding in suspension two or more different perspectives:

[T]he possible is not equated here with a new perspective—either the one added to an existing way of seeing/doing things, or the one that materializes from putting two or more perspectives together—but designates both the awareness and exploration of the space created by developing multiple instead of singular relations with the world. (Glaveanu 2020, 3)

Emerging in engagements across difference and driving both creative acts and political imaginaries, the possible—whether utopian or dystopian—is a central category of participatory sound art aesthetics. Where linear artforms offer closed definite experiences, participation thrives on instability and contingency—as well as the ephemerality of sound. Sonic gestures exchanged between participating bodies resonate the difference and facilitate the process of perspective-taking. They connect the subjects—in the already-intersubjective sense of sonic philosophy of Voegelin and Nancy—into heterogeneous assemblages that restate in aesthetic terms the political dialectics of Mouffe's antagonism and Dewey's common interest.

According to Voegelin (2019, 27), what makes sound the privileged medium of the politics of possibility is that it "offers a portal into difference and the differently real and allows us to hear alternative slices on equal track, as a real sonic fiction":

This sonic imaginary does not limit its possibility to opposition, but generates an alternative that is neither parallel, and thus without ramification and impact, nor circular, and thus incapable to leave its causality. Instead it invites a listening to the breath as a continuous resonance of otherness in a shared space. [...] Sonic fictions ... are political actions that generate a politics of possibility and transformation that outlines, with invisible lines and from a mobile depth, the condition of its narrative without sublimating the how, but illuminating its singularity and breaking its dominant echo. (Voegelin 2019, 29)

The gestures of concern, empowerment and togetherness that I discussed above—as well as many other possible gestures: of dissent, of compassion, of remediation etc.—are such sonic fictions. They drive the political imagination understood as "all those imaginative processes by which collective life is symbolically experienced and this experience mobilised in view of achieving political aims" (Glaveanu and Saint Laurent 2015, 559). Even though participatory sound art does not have the power to enact political and social change directly, it can produce, through a gestural exchange, new resonant structures and abstract narratives—new forms in Caroline Levine's (2015) terms—against which social change can take shape.

REFERENCES

Agamben, Giorgio. 1993. Notes on gesture. In *Infancy and history: Essays on the destruction of experience*, 135–140. London: Verso Books.

———. 1999. Kommerell, or on gesture. In *Potentialities: Collected essays in philosophy*, ed. Daniel Heller-Roazen, 77–85. Stanford: Stanford University Press.

Alonso, Jorge. (2005). *Marcela Lagarde: A feminist battles feminicide*. Envivo, May.

Arendt, Hannah. 1958. *The human condition*. Chicago: Chicago University Press.

Bala, Sruti. 2018. *The gestures of participatory art*. Manchester: Manchester University Press.

Baschet, François, and Bernard Baschet. 1987. Sound sculpture: Sounds, shapes, public participation, education. *Leonardo* 20: 107–114.

Bishop, Claire. 2006a. The social turn: Collaboration and its discontents. *Artforum* 44: 178–183.

———. 2006b. Introduction: Viewers as producers. In *Participation*, ed. Claire Bishop, 10–17. Cambridge, MA: MIT Press.

Bourriaud, Nicolas. (2002 [1998]). *Relational aesthetics*. Translated by Simon Pleasance and Fronza Woods. Les Presses du réel.

Butler, Judith. 2016. Rethinking vulnerability and resistance. In *Vulnerability in resistance*, ed. Judith Butler, Zeynep Gambetti, and Leticia Sabsay, 12–27. Durham, NC: Duke University Press.

Carmona, Susana Jiménez. 2020. Silences and policies in the shared listening: Ultra-red and Escuchatorio. *SoundEffects - An Interdisciplinary Journal of Sound and Sound Experience* 9: 116–131. https://doi.org/10.7146/se.v9i1.112931.

Chattopadhyay, Budhaditya. 2023. Hyper-listening and co-listening: Reflections on sound, selfhood, and solidarity. In *Sonic engagement: The ethics and aesthetics of community engaged audio practice*, ed. Sarah Woodland and Wolfgang Vachon, 158–176. Abingdon: Routledge.

Cox, Christoph, and Christina Kubisch. (2006). Invisible cities: An interview with Christina Kubisch. *Cabinet*.

Culler, Jonathan. 2015. *Theory of the lyric*. Cambridge, MA: Harvard University Press.

DeNora, Tia. 2003. *After Adorno: Rethinking music sociology*. Cambridge: Cambridge University Press.

Dewey, John. 1930 [1916]. *Democracy and education: An introduction to the philosophy of education*. New York: The Macmillan Company.

Gablik, Suzi. 1995. Connective aesthetics: Art after individualism. In *Mapping the terrain: New genre public art*, ed. Suzanne Lacy, 88–93. Seattle: Bay Press.

Giusti, Francesco. 2019. Recitation: Lyric time(s) I. In *Re-: An errant glossary*, 35–47. Berlin: ICI Berlin Press. https://doi.org/10.25620/ci-15_05.

———. 2021. Transcontextual gestures: A lyric approach to the world of literature. In *The work of world literature*, 75–103. Berlin: ICI Berlin Press. https://doi.org/10.37050/ci-19_04.

Glaveanu, Vlad Petre. 2018. Creativity in perspective: A sociocultural and critical account. *Journal of Constructivist Psychology* 31: 118–129. https://doi.org/10.1080/10720537.2016.1271376.

———. 2020. *The possible: A sociocultural theory*. Oxford: Oxford University Press.

Glaveanu, Vlad Petre, and Constance de Saint Laurent. 2015. Political imagination, otherness and the European crisis. *Europe's Journal of Psychology* 11: 557. https://doi.org/10.5964/ejop.v11i4.1085.

Gutiérrez, Amanda, and Veronica Mockler. 2022. SONO-SORO WALKS. *Tumblr*.

Heinrich, Falk. 2014. *Performing beauty in participatory art and culture*. Abingdon: Routledge.

Ingraham, Christopher. 2020. *Gestures of concern*. Durham: Duke University Press.

Kester, Grant. 2011. *The one and the many: Contemporary collaborative art in a global context*. Durham, NC: Duke University Press.

Lagarde y de los Rios, Marcela. 2006. Pacto entre mujeres: Sororidad. *Aportes*.

Levine, Caroline. 2015. *Forms: Whole, rhythm, hierarchy, network*. Princeton: Princeton University Press.

Licht, Alan. 2019. *Sound art revisited*. New York and London: Bloomsbury.

Lippard, Lucy R. 1997. *The lure of the local: Senses of place in a multicentered society*. New York: New Press.

Martin, Jack. 2005. Perspectival selves in interaction with others: Re-reading G.H. Mead's social psychology. *Journal for the Theory of Social Behaviour* 35: 231–253.

Matthews, Kaffe. 2015. *Finding Song Home*. Bicrophonic Research Institute.

———. 2020. *Enviro Bike*. Bicrophonic Research Institute.

Mead, George Herbert. 1972 [1934]. *Mind, self and society: From the standpoint of a social behaviorist*. Chicago: University of Chicago Press.

Mockus, Martha. 2007. *Sounding out: Pauline Oliveros and lesbian musicality*. Abingdon: Routledge.

Mouffe, Chantal. 2013. *Agonistics: Thinking the world politically*. London: Verso Books.

Nancy, Jean-Luc. 2007. *Listening*. New York: Fordham University Press.

Noland, Carrie. 2010. *Agency and embodiment: Performing gestures/producing culture*. Cambridge, MA: Harvard University Press.

Oliveros, Pauline. 2005. *Deep listening: A composer's sound practice*. Lincoln, NE: iUniverse.

Ouzounian, Gascia. 2013. Sound installation art. In *Music, sound and space*, ed. Georgina Born, 73–89. Cambridge: Cambridge University Press.

Polli, Andrea. 2017. Soundwalking, sonification and activism. In *Routledge companion to sounding art*, ed. Marcel Cobussen, Vincent Meelberg, and Barry Truax, 81–91. Abingdon: Routledge.

Rebelo, Pedro, and Rodrigo Cicchelli Velloso. 2018. Participatory sonic arts: The Som de Maré project—Towards a socially engaged art of sound in the everyday. In *The Routledge research companion to electronic music—Reaching out with technology*, ed. Simon Emmerson, 137–155. Abingdon: Routledge.

Rethmann, Petra. 2013. Imagining political possibility in an age of late liberalism and cynical reason. *Reviews in Anthropology* 42: 227–242.

Ryder, John. 2020. *Knowledge, art, and power: An outline of a theory of experience*. Leiden and Boston: Brill-Rodopi.

Stewart, Sharon. 2020. Inquiring into the hack: New sonic and institutional practices by Pauline Oliveros, Pussy Riot, and Goodiepal. In *The Bloomsbury handbook of sound art*, ed. Sanne Krogh Groth and Holger Schulze, 237–259. London: Bloomsbury.

Stirling, Christabel. 2016. Sound art/street life: Tracing the social and political effects of sound installations in London. *Journal of Sonic Studies* 11.

Tanaka, Atau, and Adam Parkinson. 2018. The problems with participation. In *Routledge companion to electronic music: Reaching out with technology*, ed. Simon Emmerson, 156–177. New York: Routledge.

Trondalen, Gro, and Lars Ole Bonde. 2012. Music therapy: Models and interventions. In *Music, health, and wellbeing*, ed. Raymond MacDonald, Gunter Kreutz, and Laura Mitchell, 41–62. Oxford: Oxford University Press.

Ultra-red. 2008. *10 Preliminary theses on militant sound investigation*. New York: Printed Matter, Inc.

Vandsø, Anette. 2020. The sonic aftermath: The Anthropocene and interdisciplinarity after the apocalypse. In *The Bloomsbury handbook of sound art*, ed. Sanne Krogh Groth and Holger Schulze, 19–40. London: Bloomsbury.

Voegelin, Salomé. 2010. *Listening to noise and silence: Toward a philosophy of sound art*. New York and London: Continuum.

———. 2019. *The political possibility of sound: Fragments of listening*. Bloomsbury.

Weidman, Amanda. 2015. Voice. In *Keywords in sound*, ed. David Novak and Matt Sakakeeny, 232–246. Durham, NC: Duke University Press.

CHAPTER 7

Conclusion

Abstract This chapter restates the main conclusions of the book, offering a brief summary of the Pragmatist aesthetics of participatory sound art developed in the previous chapters and discusses two fruitful directions for further research into the subject: postcolonial and posthumanist.

Keywords Pragmatism • Sound art • Postcolonial sound • Posthuman sound

As even a brief comparative overview—such as the one conducted in Chap. 2—of the histories of sound art and participatory art reveals, they arise in response to the same aesthetic and political impulses and share numerous thematic, methodological and conceptual connections. Throughout the twentieth century, the artists have turned to the ephemerality and relationality of sound as well as the contingency and sociality of participation to blur the borders between art and everyday, dissolve the art object into an art experience and question the established art institutions and social and cultural practices.

This connectedness stands in stark contrast to the widely diverging paths that sound art and participatory art discourses have taken since the two art forms were conceptualised academically and curatorially in the 1980s–2000s. An early account of sound art by the pioneering German scholar Helga de la Motte-Haber (1999) has set the tone of the discussion for the decades to come (e.g., Licht 2007; LaBelle 2015), emphasising the material—sensory, corporeal, spatial—aspects of sound. At the same time, participatory art discourse emerges from curatorial manifestos of movements such as Relational Aesthetics (Bourriaud 2002 [1998]) or New Genre Public Art (Lacy 1995) and picks up in heated academic debates of the 2000s (Bishop 2004, 2012; Kester 2004, 2011). In these texts, sociality becomes king, with the material and experiential aspects of artworks becoming secondary to the burning questions of the politics of art.

Hence, what I have attempted to do in this book is to bridge the gap between the two scholarly discourses and address the artistic practices that have fallen into it. In the preceding chapters, I have sketched an aesthetic theory of participatory sound art that addresses both materiality and sociality of this art form in equal measure. As the fundamental philosophical and epistemological differences between the sound art and participatory art discourses seem largely irreconcilable, rather than expanding one through the other, I have proposed a theoretical framework built "from scratch". It is grounded in the tradition of pragmatist philosophy, particularly John Dewey's (1980 [1934]) aesthetics and G.H. Mead's (1938, 1972 [1934]) philosophy of acts linked with the contemporary versions of pragmatism (Latour 2005; Hennion 2015; Ryder 2020). The idiosyncratic character of participatory sound art further makes it necessary to go beyond art theories proper and draws on design studies (Gibson 1979; Norman 2013) and creativity theory (Glaveanu 2010, 2013, 2015, 2018, 2020).

Let me then restate the central methodological thesis of this book: participatory sound artworks are best described neither in terms of artistic intent (whether aesthetic or political) and social impact, nor in terms of phenomenology and materiality of sound (whatever aspects one includes into these categories)—although these are all important considerations. Rather, the social-material and political-aesthetic entanglements of participatory sound are only adequately addressed through relational concepts that themselves occupy the in-between position—between the subject and the object, the material and the symbolic. In this book, I have explored three such notions: affordance, perspective and gesture. The salience of the first two is that they describe agency (creative or perceptual) as a relation: affordance refers to the opportunities for action that the artwork offers to the participants (Gibson 1979; Norman 2013), while perspective, to the way the participants' perception of these opportunities is influenced by their own past experiences and orientation to act (Martin 2005; Glaveanu 2015; Mead 1972 [1934]). Applied to participatory sound art, the two concepts reveal the many intriguing ways the materiality and sociality of artworks determine each other, while explaining the co-existence and interaction of the works' stable aesthetic structures with the contingent character of participation. The notion of the gesture then puts the focus on what happens in the participants' encounters with the artwork, while at the same time establishing a link between the participatory experience and the broader social-cultural-political context of the participants' everyday lives. On the one hand, gesture provides participatory sound art with a mechanism of corporeal, non-discursive meaning-making, being "the other side of language" (Agamben 1999, 78); on the other hand, through this corporeality, it bridges the aesthetic with the political by both manifesting a form and referring to a social function (Noland 2010; Bala 2018).

Examining the affordances of participatory sound artworks illuminates the particular ways they facilitate the audience's creativity through soundmaking and listening that are experimental, exploratory and communal, fostering the emergence of spontaneous relational assemblages glued together by sound. The focus on affordance further highlights the role of spaces, technologies and media in this process, which can be approximated through classifying artworks into three types of environments—local (technologically unextended), networked and augmented—detailing the ways their technological underpinnings influence participatory processes. At the same time, this reveals the platform-like character of participatory sound artworks, allowing to draw parallels to experimental sonic practices in participatory culture—such as the viral videos involving rubber chickens or autotune software. While not institutionally recognised as art, such practices rely on much the same affordances as participatory sound artworks in the "proper" sense.

Whereas affordances address the material conditions of participation in sound art, the notion of perspective brings the focus onto the human component. As the empirical case studies detailed in Chap. 5 show, both the artists and the participants approach the sensory aspects of the artworks as somewhat secondary to the aesthetic experience of creative soundmaking. For artists, the sonorities of their artworks are not the aesthetic goal in themselves, but rather the means of creating a social experience. On the other hand, the participants heavily prioritise their experiencing *of* making sound over expressing themselves *through* sound. In their actions and social interactions with each other in the context of the artwork, their perspectives shift, prompting them to reassess their entrenched ideas of sound and sociality, both in the context of art experience and in a broader cultural context.

Finally, the concept of the gesture—whether applied to the artworks themselves as artistic gestures or to the (possible) actions of the participants—draws a link between the aesthetic experience of participatory sound artworks and their politics. Considering the three most prominent types of gestures in participatory sound art—of concern, empowerment and togetherness—points to a continuality between critical and remediational forms of sound art's politics. The notion of the gesture allows to avoid the double trap of reducing the politics of art to either clearly stated artistic intent or quantifiable effect (Bala 2018). Instead, it reveals a post-critical (Felski 2015) sensibility in sound art, operating politically through operating affectively and aesthetically. Rather than laying bare "matters of fact" and forgone conclusions, performing sonic gestures offers the participants a first-person and visceral perspective on the political issues at hand and fosters empowerment through creating a sense of community while sustaining difference.

This account of affordances, perspectives and gestures of participatory sound art, however, is far from being complete and exhaustive. Rather this book should be approached as an attempt to open up the discussion on participation in sound art and offer some initial observations. In this spirit, I would like to conclude by considering the paths not taken: possible directions for further research that may have been hinted at but not explored in the previous chapters.

To an extent, these openings follow directly from the limitations of my study. Analysing participatory artworks is largely impossible without directly engaging with them both materially and socially. As a Russian scholar living and working in Northern Europe, the corpus of artworks available to me is limited by my geographical circumstances and the languages I speak. Due to these constraints, I have chosen to focus my research on participatory sound art from the (broadly understood) Western art world. Although a broader geographical context is hinted at in the historical overview in Chap. 2, which includes brief discussions of sound and participation in Russian avantgarde and of Brazilian Neoconcrete artists, this is primarily because of their importance to the histories of sound and participation in the West. Similarly, I have attempted to include the works by non-Western sound artists and/or artists of colour in the discussion in Chaps. 4 and 6, but their selection is once again limited to artworks circulating in the European art context or on the internet. At the same time, a decolonial urgency emerges in sound studies of recent years exemplified, e.g., in the special issues of *Journal of Sonic Studies* on sound in South-East Asia (vol. 12), Latin America (vol. 19) or the Balkans (vol. 23), monographs such as *Hungry Listening* (Robinson 2020) or *Africa in Stereo: Modernism, Music, and Pan-African Solidarity* (Jaji 2014), anthologies *Remapping Sound Studies* (Steingo and Sykes 2019), *Making It Heard: A History of Brazilian Sound Art* (Chaves and Iazzetta 2019), *Indian Sound Cultures, Indian Sound Citizenship* (Brueck et al. 2020) or Budhaditya Chattopadhyay's (2022) collection of interviews *Sound Practices in the Global South*.

These works speak to the importance of opening up the research of participatory sound art studies to include the artists and practices of the Global South. I want to consider briefly two examples that speak to this urgency. In her chapter "'Diam!' (Be Quiet!): Noisy Sound Art from the Global South" in the *Bloomsbury Handbook of Sound Art*, Sanne Krogh Groth (2020) offers a comparative account of the performances of Indonesian artists at the CTM festival in Berlin and at various events in Java. She observes that the practices of the Indonesian experimental music and sound scene are rather similar to that of European Avantgarde, as they build on the musical traditions and conventions of their culture, renegotiating and subverting them into something new. According to Groth, this paradigmatic similarity is what partly explains the success of these artists in the West. However, unlike the Western art music that has served as the point of departure and the foil to Western sound art, the traditions on which Indonesian artists build are themselves participatory rather than presentational performances in Turino's (2008) terms. Experimental bands such as Senyawa or Gabber Modus Operandi, for example, make frequent references to traditional ritual dances as influence for their sonic practices—dances, which remain part of everyday culture in Indonesia (Novak 2016; Rohlf 2019). Groth (2020, 117) thus points to a certain disconnect between the music and the way it was situated at CTM: in traditional theatrical black boxes, with professional sound systems and full control over the action, where "less attention was paid to the situated, the social, and the discursive, in favor of presentations of autonomous aesthetics". She contrasts these performances with the underground events she had visited in Java where "the audience supported the artists and brought energy to the [performance] by commenting and slam-dancing around, sometimes even with the musicians" (Krogh Groth 2020, 118). In other words, the same sonic practices and forms were approached as presentational in the Global North and participatory in the Global South. This contrast makes tangible the cultural embeddedness and conditionality of both sound art's affordances and the participants' perspectives. It makes clear the necessity of rethinking participation, sound and listening from a decolonial perspective—but also highlights the importance of considering participation in the study of sonic practices in the Global South.

The second text I want to discuss here is Hadi Bastani's (2020) article "Experimental Electronic Sound as Playful Articulation of a Compromised Sociality in Iran". Bastani traces the emergence of the Iranian experimental electronics scene in 2010s—originating as part of online participatory culture and later spilling into physical spaces and live performances. Western commentators (e.g., Mitchell 2016) have criticised this scene, comparing it unfavourably to underground Iranian pop, for its abstract aesthetic and a lack of explicit political messaging. Bastani (2020) retorts, however, that such claims would be ignorant of the local context. He argues that the playful aesthetic of experimental sound, not subjected to compositional rules and traditions, can in itself be heard as a form of political resistance to the ubiquitous and pervasive forms of state control over moral, legal and ethical issues. Experimental sound thus provides an outlet for the political subjectivity urging to escape the "deep-rooted mechanisms of dogmatic ethical-moral judgement, crystallised for instance through the laws but also citizens' self-policing and policing of each other" (Bastani 2020, 391).

Bastani's study hints simultaneously at two fruitful venues for further research of participatory sound art. First is the decolonisation of the politics of art—a rethinking of what kinds of gestures could and should be understood as political and the cultural situatedness of their functioning as such. Second, he discusses how participating in international online communities of experimental soundmakers equipped Iranian artists—both trained musicians and amateurs—"with new imaginaries that enable alternative modes of sociality performed outside the reach and control of 'traditional' authorities like the central government or nuclear family" (Bastani 2020, 388). This further opens up the question about the role of participatory culture and online communities in driving forward both the aesthetics and politics of sound art in the globalised world.

At the same time, a growing corpus of New Materialist and Posthumanist texts, both on sound art (Cecchetto 2013; Cox 2018) and in general (e.g., Bennett 2009; Kohn 2013; Morton 2013; Harris 2021), has drawn attention to the issues of sociality and politics of non-humans. My book, however, has a distinctly human focus, dictated by its main goal is to bring attention to participation in the traditional sense of the word. It does address non-human agency in participatory sound art to an extent, using the notions of mediation and affordance to explore the material agencies of the artworks and the ways they interact with the human agencies. But there is also a potential for expanding the category of participation itself to include a variety of non-human actors such as robots, animals or natural forces on equal footing with human participants. Let me briefly consider three examples that illustrate these possibilities: Céleste Boursier-Mougenot's *from here to ear,* John Cayley's *The Listeners* and Gordon Monahan's Aeolian sound installations.

From here to ear (1999–) is a series of sound installations that creates within the exhibition space an artificial environment for a flock of finches, which includes a number of amplified musical instruments—typically, electric guitars and drums. As the birds go about their daily business, they inevitably interact with the instruments, creating a kind of continuous improvised music piece that interweaves birdsong and instrumental sounds. In other words, the finches co-create the work in much the same ways as the human participants in many of the projects discussed in this book: they act upon the sonic affordances offered to them by the materialities of the artwork, necessitating an expanded notion of participation. As Martin Ullrich and Sebastian Trump (2023, 35) argue in their article "Sonic Collaborations between Humans, Non-human Animals and Artificial Intelligences", "if socially engaged art practices are defined as taking human relations and their social contexts as points of departure, such a definition seems to be inherently anthropocentric. It puts its emphasis on human relations and thus implicitly excludes all non-human agents." In *from here to ear*, the sound emerges as the result of such a non-human sociality—or more precisely, an interspecies one, as the birds react to the gallery visitors as well, who thus indirectly affect their soundmaking. At the same time, the fundamental difference of such non-human participation is the bird's inability to give informed consent to it, bringing a whole new dimension to the questions of the ethics of participation and of the border between participation and exploitation. Investigating the animal welfare in a number of art project, including a version of *from here to ear* at the Queensland Gallery of Modern Art, Amanda Pagliarino (2021, 34, 39) observes that "at the conclusion of presentations in 2010 and 2016, a greater number of birds were returned to the homes of the [Queensland Finch Society] aviculturists than had arrived at GOMA, due to successful breeding within the colonies", which "indicated that the finches were exhibiting natural behaviours, the colonies were stable and the environment inside GOMA was favourable". In other words, the birds were not harmed and even thrived in the installation environment. Pagliarino (2021) notes, however, that as the attitudes towards animal rights develop, the animal welfare may become no longer a sufficient factor to deem animal participation ethical.

The other—and the more headline-grabbing—line in the field of Posthuman artmaking is machine creativity. In some ways, the use of robots and robot-like mechanisms in sound art is nothing new: one needs only to think back to Joe Jones' musical machines, or even to the Baroque music-playing automatons. The recent advances in machine learning, however, have made artificial creativity a hot topic, with some artists and musicians worried that AI will soon come to replace them, while others such as Jennifer Walshe or Tomomi Adachi, readily embracing the creative possibilities of the new tech.

The two reactions map neatly onto two approaches to AI creativity: one tracing back to Alan Turing and presenting the AI as an autonomous creator made in the image of a human; the other, as Oscar Schwartz (2018) points out, drawing on the lesser-known proposal for AI as human-machine collaboration, or even "symbiosis", by another classic of computer science, J.C.R. Licklider (1960). Both approaches have implications for the definition of participation: if we consider AIs as autonomous entities, they can participate in sound artworks same as humans, while as collaborations, they are themselves inherently participatory. Moreover, the two approaches are not even necessarily mutually exclusive. Case in point: *The Listeners* (2015–) is a sound poetry—or "aurature" (Cayley 2017)—work by the Canadian poet and digital artist John Cayley that exists in several forms: as a performance, a gallery installation, an audio recording and a smartphone app. At its core is an extension—a "skill"—for Amazon Echo apps and devices that enable the user to enter a poetic dialog with Amazon's voice assistant Alexa through its speech recognition and voice synthesis capabilities. The script is interactive and flexible, weaving together pre-written fragments with lines generated in real time in response to the user's questions and statements—in other words, engaging both the user and Alexa as participants in the work with their creative agencies and perspectives. After all, as N. Katherine Hayles (2005) argues, subjecthood is closely tied to agency; when a machine can exercise the latter, it stands to reason to expect it to exhibit a degree of the former—and therefore to have a perspective.

Finally, whereas we are used to ascribe a degree of personhood and agency to animals and AIs (since the former are sentient and the latter can convincingly emulate sentience), extending the notion of participation to natural forces may seem like a stretch—unless under a kind of animist epistemology. However, a certain parallelism may be found in the way the artist constructs the affordances of the artwork and the way these affordances are acted upon between works involving human participation and those of winds and water streams. Since the 1980s, the Canadian sound artist Gordon Monahan has realised a number of installations that played on the Aeolian effect—the excitement of sonic vibrations in strings under the force of wind. For example, in *Aeolian Winds Over Claybank Saskatchewan* (2006/2007) he stretched long piano wires in a net between the various towers and of the Claybank Brick Factory heritage site. Depending on the direction and force of the wind, the strings produced different combinations of harmonic tones. Put differently, the artist essentially created an instrument for the wind to play—much like the Baschets created their sound sculptures for the audience to play, or Boursier-Mougenot created his sound installations for the finches to play. The relational nature of affordances does not require a distinction between living and non-living actors, just like it does not require a distinction between human and animal ones.

How would one go to address the creative agencies of wind, water currents, light or gravity? In his book *How Forests Think*, Eduardo Kohn (2013) puts forward a project of the "anthropology beyond the human", questioning the assumption of social sciences that representation, assumed to be the basis of thought and creativity, is a uniquely human trait. He draws on Perice's semiotics to demonstrate how "nonsymbolic representational modalities" (Kohn 2013, 8) permeate the non-human—and even non-living—world and can thus be explored through ethnographic methods. When speaking of semiosis of water currents or rock formations, Kohn (2013, 20) proposes addressing through the notion of form— "strange but nonetheless worldly process of pattern production and propagation" that can be observed in a variety of phenomena from rock formation to vegetation growth to social forms in animals and humans and that is "neither mind nor mechanism". Furthermore,

Rethinking cause through form forces us to rethink agency as well. What is this strange way of getting something done without doing anything at all? What kinds of politics can come into being through this particular way of creating associations? (Kohn 2013, 21)

Kohn's proposition evokes Caroline Levine's (2015) account of forms as structures that easily travel between the social and the aesthetic, making them into a category that operates across the whole continuum of human and non-human participation. His opening of the ethnographic method towards the non-human and non-living thus offers a way to explore the creative agencies, perspectives and political gestures of such—the same way this book employed traditional ethnographic methods to study human participants.

This brief overview of the two possible ways to open up the category of participation in sound art, the postcolonial and the posthuman, reveals it to be broad and flexible concept that is salient to a far larger corpus of artworks than the traditional understanding of participation in the Western art discourse suggests and that was discussed in this book. Hopefully, however, it has also demonstrated that the pragmatist framework offered here is robust enough to address such an opening up.

References

Agamben, Giorgio. 1999. Kommerell, or on gesture. In *Potentialities: Collected essays in philosophy*, ed. Daniel Heller-Roazen, 77–85. Stanford: Stanford University Press.

Bala, Sruti. 2018. *The gestures of participatory art*. Manchester: Manchester University Press.

Bastani, Hadi. 2020. Experimental electronic sound as playful articulation of a compromised sociality in Iran. *Ethnomusicology Forum* 29: 379–400. https://doi.org/10.1080/17411912.2021.1896371.

Bennett, Jane. 2009. *Vibrant matter: A political ecology of things*. Durham, NC: Duke University Press.

Bishop, Claire. 2004. Antagonism and relational aesthetics. *October* 110: 51–79. https://doi.org/10.1162/0162287042379810.

———. 2012. *Artificial hells: Participatory art and the politics of spectatorship*. London: Verso Books.

Bourriaud, Nicolas. 2002 [1998]. *Relational aesthetics*. Translated by Simon Pleasance and Fronza Woods. Les Presses du réel.

Brueck, Laura, Jacob Smith, and Neil Verma. 2020. *Indian sound cultures, Indian sound citizenship*. Ann Arbor, MI: University of Michigan Press.
Cayley, John. 2017. The advent of aurature and the end of (electronic) literature. In *The Bloomsbury handbook of electronic literature*, ed. Joseph Tabbi, 73–92. London: Bloomsbury.
Cecchetto, David. 2013. *Humanesis: Sound and technological Posthumanism*. University of Minnesota Press.
Chattopadhyay, Budhaditya. 2022. *Sound practices in the global south: Co-listening to resounding plurilogues*. London: Palgrave Macmillan.
Chaves, Rui, and Fernando Iazzetta, eds. 2019. *Making it heard: A history of Brazilian sound art*. New York: Bloomsbury.
Cox, Christoph. 2018. *Sonic flux: Sound, art and metaphysics*. Chicago: University of Chicago Press.
Dewey, John. 1980 [1934]. *Art as experience*. New York: Perigee Books.
Felski, Rita. 2015. *The limits of critique*. Chicago: University of Chicago Press.
Gibson, James Jerome. 1979. *The ecological approach to visual perception*. Boston, MA: Houghton Mifflin.
Glaveanu, Vlad Petre. 2010. Paradigms in the study of creativity: Introducing the perspective of cultural psychology. *New Ideas in Psychology* 28: 79–93.
———. 2013. Rewriting the language of creativity: The five A's framework. *Review of General Psychology* 17: 69–81. https://doi.org/10.1037/a0029528.
———. 2015. Creativity as a sociocultural act. *The Journal of Creative Behavior* 49: 165–180.
———. 2018. Creativity in perspective: A sociocultural and critical account. *Journal of Constructivist Psychology* 31: 118–129. https://doi.org/10.108 0/10720537.2016.1271376.
———. 2020. *The possible: A sociocultural theory*. Oxford: Oxford University Press.
Harris, Dan. 2021. *Creative agency*. London: Springer Nature.
Hayles, N. Katherine. 2005. *My mother was a computer: Digital subjects and literary texts*. Chicago: University of Chicago Press.
Hennion, Antoine. 2015. *The passion for music: A sociology of mediation*. Farnham: Ashgate.
Jaji, Tsitsi Ella. 2014. *Africa in stereo: Modernism, music, and pan-African solidarity*. Oxford University Press.
Kester, Grant. 2004. *Conversation pieces: Community and communication in modern art*. Berkeley, CA: University of California Press.
———. 2011. *The one and the many: Contemporary collaborative art in a global context*. Durham, NC: Duke University Press.
Kohn, Eduardo. 2013. *How forests think: Toward an anthropology beyond the human*. UC Press.

Krogh Groth, Sanne. 2020. "Diam!" (be quiet!): Noisy sound art from the global south. In *The Bloomsbury handbook of sound art*, ed. Sanne Krogh Groth and Holger Schulze, 107–120. Bloomsbury Handbooks. Bloomsbury Academic.

LaBelle, Brandon. 2015. *Background noise: Perspectives on sound art*. 2nd ed. New York: Bloomsbury.

Lacy, Suzanne, ed. 1995. *Mapping the terrain: New genre public art*. Seattle: Bay Press.

Latour, Bruno. 2005. *Reassembling the social: An introduction to actor-network-theory*. Oxford: Oxford University Press.

Levine, Caroline. 2015. *Forms: Whole, rhythm, hierarchy, network*. Princeton: Princeton University Press.

Licht, Alan. 2007. *Sound art: Beyond music, between categories*. New York: Rizzoli; Har/Com edition.

Licklider, J.C.R. 1960. Man-computer symbiosis. *IRE Transactions on Human Factors in Electronics* 1: 4–11.

Martin, Jack. 2005. Perspectival selves in interaction with others: Re-reading G.H. Mead's social psychology. *Journal for the Theory of Social Behaviour* 35: 231–253.

Mead, George Herbert. 1938. *The philosophy of the act*. Chicago: University of Chicago Press.

———. 1972 [1934]. *Mind, self and society: From the standpoint of a social behaviorist*. Chicago: University of Chicago Press.

Mitchell, Tony. 2016. Absence: A survey of music from Iran. *Cyclic Defrost*, March 21.

Morton, Timothy. 2013. *Hyperobjects: Philosophy and ecology after the end of the world*. Minneapolis: University of Minnesota Press.

Motte-Haber, Helga de la, ed. 1999. *Klangkunst: tönende Objekte und klingende Räume*. Laaber: Laaber-Verlag.

Noland, Carrie. 2010. *Agency and embodiment: Performing gestures/producing culture*. Cambridge, MA: Harvard University Press.

Norman, Donald A. 2013. *The design of everyday things: Revised and expanded edition*. London: Hachette UK.

Novak, David. 2016. Bomb: Senyawa by David Novak. *BOMB Magazine*, August 10.

Pagliarino, Amanda. 2021. A measure of happiness—The use of live animals in contemporary art installations. *AICCM Bulletin* 42: 26–42. https://doi.org/10.1080/10344233.2021.1989257.

Robinson, Dylan. 2020. *Hungry listening: Resonant theory for indigenous sound studies*. University of Minnesota Press.

Rohlf, Jan. 2019. BPM orgasm Club music. Gabber modus operandi in conversation with Jan Rohlf. In *CTM 2019: Persistence Magazine*, ed. Oliver Baurhenn, Jan Rohlf, and Remco Schuurbiers, 66–71. Berlin: Disk.

Ryder, John. 2020. *Knowledge, art, and power: An outline of a theory of experience*. Leiden and Boston: Brill-Rodopi.

Schwartz, Oscar. 2018. Competing visions for AI: Turing, Licklider and generative literature. *Digital Culture & Society* 4: 87–106. https://doi.org/10.14361/dcs-2018-0107.

Steingo, Gavin, and Jim Sykes. 2019. *Remapping sound studies*. Durham, NC: Duke University Press.

Turino, Thomas. 2008. *Music as social life: The politics of participation*. Chicago: University of Chicago Press.

Ullrich, Martin, and Sebastian Trump. 2023. Sonic collaborations between humans, non-human animals and artificial intelligences: Contemporary and future aesthetics in more-than-human worlds. *Organised Sound* 28. 35–42. https://doi.org/10.1017/S1355771822000097.

Index[1]

A
Acoustic community, 37, 46, 71
Act
  creative act, 7, 58–60, 68, 84, 102, 132
  sound act, 3, 29, 48, 54–56, 106–107
Actor-network theory, 5, 58, 102
Aesthetics, 4, 32, 44, 46–48, 50–53, 57, 61, 90, 100, 118, 130, 132, 137–139, 141, 142
  aesthetic experience, 3, 29, 50, 51, 53, 55–56, 66, 72, 73, 82, 84, 85, 105, 108, 139, 140
Affordance, 5, 6, 57–59, 61, 67–71, 74, 78, 81, 84, 86, 93, 100, 117, 126, 129, 130, 138–140, 142, 143, 145
  for connectivity, 6, 7, 66, 68, 70–71, 76, 84, 86, 126, 129, 130
  for creativity, 3, 4, 6, 7, 22, 24, 36, 44, 45, 57, 59, 66–68, 83–85, 90, 93–96, 98, 101, 102, 105, 106, 111, 131, 138, 139, 144, 145
  for exploration and experimentation, 6, 7, 38, 39, 66, 68–70, 80, 83, 84, 86, 120, 126, 132
Agamben, Giorgio, 6, 56, 117, 139
Agency, 5–8, 14, 15, 25, 29, 33, 45, 46, 50, 52–55, 57–61, 74, 76, 80, 84, 90–91, 93, 98, 102, 104, 105, 111, 116, 118, 119, 122, 125, 138, 143–146
  creative agency, 7, 14, 15, 57, 61, 67, 82, 85, 90–92, 100, 102, 103, 110, 116, 144–146
Ainsworth, Esther, 131
Amacher, Maryanne, 77
Antagonism, 23, 48, 53, 81, 119, 121, 122, 131, 132
Arendt, Hannah, 127

---

[1] Note: Page numbers followed by 'n' refer to notes.

Art
  autonomy of art, 48, 51
  object, 4, 24, 29, 32, 35, 36, 47, 50, 66, 137
  politics of art, 3, 4, 8, 11, 46, 47, 49, 51–54, 56, 57, 61, 81, 85, 101, 106, 116–120, 123, 125, 127–129, 131, 132, 137–140, 142, 146
  production, 4, 5, 32, 33, 44, 46, 57, 59, 70, 118, 145
  reception, 2, 4, 5, 50, 70, 111
Audio recording, 13, 56, 72, 83, 125, 126, 128, 129, 144
Autotune, 83
Avantgarde
  historical, 4, 22–24, 22n1
  Post-war, 4, 22, 24–30, 35
Avraamov, Arseny, 24, 24n2

B
Bala, Sruti, 6, 8, 56, 90, 118, 119, 124, 139, 140
Barri, Tarik, 38, 69
Baschet, Bernard and François, 1, 2, 25, 67, 69, 72, 106, 116, 126
Belmore, Rebecca, 127, 128
Bertoia, Harry, 2, 25, 75
Beuys, Joseph, 26, 30, 36, 100
Bishop, Claire, 3, 4, 14, 22n1, 23, 24, 32, 35, 48, 49, 51, 53, 54, 90, 124, 138
Born, Georgina, 5, 38, 59, 71
Bourriaud, Nicolas, 32, 33, 35, 47, 130, 138

C
Cage, John, 11, 27, 30, 35, 49, 100, 101
Cardiff, Janet, 74, 81
Chattopadhyay, Budhaditya, 129, 141
Clark, Lygia, 25, 30

Collins, Karen, 38, 55, 56, 82
Community, 8, 12, 33, 37, 38, 46, 52, 53, 107–110, 123, 125–127, 129–131, 140
Cox, Christoph, 10, 44, 116, 142

D
Dadaism, 100
DeNora, Tia, 12, 58, 117
Dewey, John, 5, 16, 50–53, 57, 66, 84, 129, 131, 132, 138
Dezeuze, Anna, 14, 15, 25
Digital age, 4, 23, 82
Digital culture, 4

E
Eco, Umberto, 12, 29, 90
Environment, 5–7, 26, 37, 45, 46, 50, 52, 57, 58, 60, 66, 69, 71–82, 85, 86, 92, 95, 106, 107, 120, 125, 130, 139, 143
  augmented, 6, 36, 66, 69, 72, 73, 78, 79, 86, 120, 124, 125, 139
  local, 6, 66, 72–75, 77, 79, 85, 86, 120, 129, 131, 139
  networked, 6, 37, 66, 72, 73, 75–77, 82, 86, 139
Escuchatorio, 128–130
Experience, 3, 5, 8, 10, 14, 15, 25, 29, 36, 38, 46–48, 50–57, 60, 68, 69, 74, 75, 79–82, 84, 86, 93, 96–98, 101, 102, 105, 107–111, 116, 118, 120–122, 124, 125, 128, 132, 138, 139
  art experience, 5, 48, 50, 53, 57, 81, 83, 137, 140
  sensory experience, 3, 4, 6, 45, 47, 49, 51, 52, 54, 78, 101, 120, 138, 139

F

Faber, Katrine, 7, 91–98, 106, 110, 117
Felski, Rita, 51, 90, 140
Form, 51, 58, 61, 66, 67, 107–109, 118, 133, 139, 145, 146

G

Gablik, Suzi, 32, 33, 47, 122
Gesamtkunstwerk, 4, 21–23
Gesture, 5, 8, 53–57, 61, 74, 75, 99, 101, 116–126, 128–132, 138, 140, 142, 146
   of concern, 4, 8, 54, 102, 107, 118–123, 125, 126, 129, 131, 132, 140
   of empowerment, 8, 118, 119, 123–129, 131, 132, 140
   of togetherness, 8, 118, 128–132, 140
   unsolicited, 56, 118, 119
Gibson, James, 5, 58, 59, 138
Glaveanu, Vlad, 7, 57, 60, 90, 95, 96, 100, 102, 121, 131, 132, 138
Gutiérrez, Amanda, 124, 125, 129

H

Heinrich, Falk, 3, 53, 54, 118
Hennion, Antoine, 5, 12, 59, 138
Hinde, Kathy, 68

I

Immersion, 35, 80, 85
Interaction, 3, 5, 6, 15, 26, 33, 46–48, 50, 53–56, 58, 66, 67, 70–72, 75, 81, 82, 85, 91, 100–105, 109, 118, 126, 130, 139

K

Kahn, Douglas, 11, 12, 30, 36, 44
Kester, Grant, 3, 8, 14, 47, 48, 51, 53, 54, 107, 116, 138

Kim-Cohen, Seth, 11, 12, 27, 44, 49, 86, 90, 101
Klangkunst, 9, 30
Krogh Groth, Sanne, 2, 10, 59, 103, 141
Kubisch, Christina, 79, 86, 116

L

LaBelle, Brandon, 2, 3, 10, 12, 15, 46, 48, 49, 70, 86, 138
Latour, Bruno, 5, 8, 58, 102, 103, 138
Levine, Caroline, 51, 58, 118, 133, 146
Licht, Alan, 2, 3, 7, 10, 11, 24, 30, 45, 106, 122, 129, 138
Listening, 1, 3, 6, 10, 13, 15, 33, 38, 44–47, 50, 55, 68, 69, 71–75, 77, 79–81, 85, 86, 96, 101, 106–108, 110, 111, 116, 122, 123, 125, 128–130, 132, 139, 142
Lockwood, Annea, 29

M

Materiality, 3, 12, 16, 22, 25, 26, 29, 30, 35, 46, 48, 56, 71, 72, 75, 82, 107, 138, 139, 143
Matthews, Kaffe, 67, 69, 71, 79, 80, 120, 121, 124
Maubrey, Benoît, 7, 76, 82, 91, 99–102, 106, 117
Mead, George Herbert, 5, 7, 53, 54, 56, 59, 60, 108, 121, 138
Media art, 3, 26, 35, 36, 66
Mediality, 6, 49, 51, 53–55, 66, 72, 107
Mediation, 5, 57–59, 66, 77, 102–105, 107, 111, 143
   mediator, 47, 59, 61, 72, 103, 105, 117

Merleau-Ponty, Maurice, 25, 44
Microsound, 37, 38
Mockler, Veronica, 124, 125
Motte-Haber, Helga de la, 2, 3, 9, 10, 30, 31, 137
Mouffe, Chantal, 52, 131, 132
Music, 2, 4, 7–15, 23, 24, 30, 31, 37, 38, 44, 45, 55, 57, 59, 67, 72, 74–76, 80, 90, 92, 94, 97, 99–101, 103, 104, 107–111, 117, 118, 122, 123, 126, 129, 130, 141, 143, 144
Musical instrument, 1, 26, 38, 44, 143

N
Nehls, Anselm, 38, 69
Neuhaus, Max, 1, 2, 29, 30, 37, 67, 71, 72, 74, 75, 79, 106
New Genre Public Art, 32, 138
New materialism, 4, 5, 44, 50
Noise orchestra, 24
Non-human, 3, 57, 59, 61, 84, 90, 102, 116, 122, 143, 145, 146

O
O+A (Bruce Odland and Sam Auinger), 74
Oliveros, Pauline, 28, 122–124, 126, 129
  Deep Listening, 122, 123
Ouzounian, Gascia, 11, 12, 46, 127

P
Participation, 1–9, 11–16, 21–35, 39, 44, 47–51, 53–56, 59, 61, 66, 67n1, 72n2, 76, 78, 81, 85, 86, 90–92, 94, 99–111, 116, 118–120, 122, 124, 128, 129, 132, 137, 139, 140, 142–146

collaboration, 14–16, 46, 48, 71, 85, 128, 129, 144
interactivity, 2–4, 14–16, 35, 55, 66, 73, 120
participatory art, 3–5, 8, 14–16, 21–24, 22n1, 27, 29, 30, 32, 36, 37, 39, 44, 47–51, 53, 54, 56, 57, 60, 61, 66, 68, 82, 84, 90, 91, 119, 123, 129, 130, 137, 138, 140, 141; invitation, 93, 95, 96, 103, 104, 111, 119
participatory culture, 7, 13, 37–39, 66, 83, 139, 142
Performance, 2, 7, 12, 13, 15, 24, 26, 28, 54, 56, 68, 73, 78, 86, 91–94, 96–98, 108–110, 117, 141, 144
Performativity, 7, 11, 54, 55, 68, 76, 98, 101, 111, 119, 120, 124, 130, 140
Perspective (Mead), 5, 7, 46, 49–51, 59–61, 80, 90–92, 94–98, 100–103, 105, 106, 108–111, 118, 121, 122, 128, 131, 132, 138–140, 142, 145, 146
  action-orientation, 6, 60, 90, 93, 98
  perspective-taking, 60, 96, 102, 105, 118, 132
Phenomenology, 4, 5, 10, 25, 44, 47, 49–51, 53, 54, 138
Phillips, Liz, 2, 73, 75
Politics of the possible, 8, 131
Postcritique, 51
Pragmatism, 4, 5, 14, 44, 49–53, 61, 84, 138, 146
  doing and undergoing, 3, 5, 50, 53–61, 69, 70, 84, 93, 106, 116, 121, 124, 132, 146
  pragmatist aesthetics, 5, 50, 51, 53, 61, 84
Public art, 57, 130
Public space, 61, 71, 74, 76, 77, 81, 91, 103, 105, 119, 121, 122, 124, 127, 131

R

Rebelo, Pedro, 16, 76, 107, 128
Relationality, 6, 11, 32, 46, 47, 50, 53, 58, 60, 70–72, 96, 122, 128, 130, 137–139, 145
 relational aesthetics, 32, 47, 130, 138
Rueb, Teri, 80
Russolo, Luigi, 23
Ryder, John, 52, 53, 131, 138

S

Schafer, R.M., 27, 45, 95, 96
Schulze, Holger, 2, 10, 60, 68
Sociality, 3, 9–13, 22, 29, 35, 45, 47, 49, 51, 55, 70, 84–86, 107, 109, 129, 137–140, 142, 143
Sonic memes, 7, 38, 83
Sonic persona, 60
Sound art
 participatory sound art, 3–8, 13–16, 22, 39, 44, 49, 51, 53–56, 59–61, 66, 67, 69–71, 83–85, 90, 91, 106, 111, 116–122, 126, 128, 131, 132, 138–143, 146
 sound artist, 2, 7, 11, 39, 60, 91, 106, 107, 111, 129, 140, 145
 sound installation, 2, 9, 11, 15, 29, 37, 39, 46, 48, 49, 56, 59, 68, 69, 73–75, 79, 80, 107, 127, 143, 145
 sound in the arts, 11, 12, 31
 soundscape, 27, 36, 37, 45, 46, 74, 78–80, 91, 93, 95–97, 99, 125, 131
 sound sculpture, 2, 9, 15, 25, 26, 29, 38, 58, 67, 71, 73, 75, 76, 83, 100, 106, 126, 145
 soundwalk, 2, 16, 27, 46, 68, 69, 71, 73, 79–81, 107, 124, 125

Soundmaking, 3, 7, 13, 15, 26, 36, 44, 55, 59, 61, 68–74, 77, 81, 86, 100, 101, 103–105, 108, 111, 116, 118, 139, 143
Spatiality, 6, 9, 11, 12, 29, 30, 44–47, 68–70, 72–74, 81, 85, 96, 103, 138
Stirling, Christabel, 49, 119, 129, 131

T

Tanaka, Atau, 78, 107, 119, 124
Technology, 3–7, 29, 35–38, 44, 46, 47, 59, 66, 72, 73, 75, 76, 78–86, 91, 100, 102, 103, 105, 116, 128, 130, 139
Therapy, 126
TikTok, 84
Truax, Barry, 27, 37, 45, 46, 71
Turino, Thomas, 12, 13, 108–110, 141
Twitter, 38, 39, 70, 77, 82, 99, 100, 105

U

Ultra-red, 116

V

Voegelin, Salomé, 3, 10, 12, 13, 15, 44, 45, 49, 50, 122, 128, 131, 132
Vogel, Peter, 2, 26, 30, 75
Voice, 37, 44, 77, 83, 96–99, 104, 111, 120, 125, 127, 128, 144

W

Westerkamp, Hildegard, 2, 27

Printed in the United States
by Baker & Taylor Publisher Services